The Novels of
Manju Kapur and Jai Nimbkar
A Study in Women's Emancipation

The Novels of Manju Kapur and Jai Nimbkar
A Study in Women's Emancipation

P. Babitha Vivekavathi

Prestige Books International
New Delhi

Published by
Prestige Books International
New Delhi 110 060
prestigebooks@gmail.com
Phone: 9818755529

Associate Office
Sydney 2001

ISBN: 978-81-947512-5-0

Printed in India

Contents

Preface

Women's writing in English has entered a new phase of representation of a New Indian Woman. During recent decades, umpteen Indian women writers have written with the self-imposed task of representing the women's problems in a style that is away from the earlier stereotyped writers. After World War II, women writers have begun to come out of their grotto and address the world from their vantage point. They do not stand in the patriarchal circle of confinement and are dissatisfied with the inhibiting cultural, natural and sexual roles imposed on them by patriarchal society. The new woman of the Indian English novel views herself as the object of cultural/ social oppressions and attempts to rebel against them, consciously or unconsciously, within her living space. The characteristic features of women writers not only articulate woman's voice but also critique the canons of patriarchy. Their ideas are based on exploration of biological differences. They scrutinize the position of woman in the male dominated social context.

The early decades of twentieth century witnessed an improvement in position of woman due to the reform movements led by Raja Ram Mohun Roy, Dayanand Saraswati, Jyotiba Phule, Savitribai Phule and Dr. B.R. Ambedkar. Mahatma Gandhi's emphasis on women's participation in his non-violent moment also contributed to the change. Fiction writing by Indian women brought about maturity in the educated women of India. Publication of novels by Kamala Markandeya, Ruth Prawer Jhabvala, Nayantara Sahgal, Shashi Deshpande, Anita Desai, Kiran Desai, Uma Vasudev, Githa Hariharan, Shobha De, Arundati Roy, Manju Kapur, Jai Nimbkar, Chitra Banerjee Divakaruni, Gita Mehta and others has accelerated the process of women consciousness. These novelists have explored the plight of modern Indian woman who paved the way to liberate her form the male-dominated society.

These women writers portray the man-woman relationship in the context of modern education and their social consciousness. Their protagonists come out of the shell of male domination and establish their identity. They are no longer meek and submissive; they articulate boldly their feelings, emotions, aspirations and achievements which pave way to emancipation of women in the family in general and the relations between wife and husband in particular. Among the recent novelists, Manju Kapur and Jai Nimbkar stand apart with their skillful presentation of this theme of emancipation in women in their fiction.

A brief review of criticism on Manju Kapur and Jai Nimbkar reveals perspective on liberation of woman, Man-Woman relationships, cross-cultural conflict, self-realization, gender discrimination, etc. Critics like Sarabjit Sandhu, Sarla Palkar, Kavya, R.K. Dhawan, Suman Bala, Prasanna Sree, Indira Bhatt and R.S. Pathak have studies from the perspectives of the postcolonial and postmodernism, no substantial attempt has been made so far to focus attention on emancipation of woman in modern times. The present study will attempt to fill that gap

Before closing these remarks, I will like to record my deep sense of gratitude to my supervisor, Dr. B. Krishnaiah, Assistant professor, School of Humanities, University of Hyderabad, for his cheerful readiness to spare his valuable time to guide my research work. His critical approach, inspiring suggestions and sustained encouragement have not only made my task easier but also helped me in giving a shape to my thesis.

I express my profound thanks to Professor K. Sayanna, the Vice Chancellor, Professor K. Purushotham, the Registrar, Professor V. Srinivas, Dean, Faculty of Arts, Dr. M. Prabhakar, Head, Department of English, Dr. Deepa Jyothi, Chairman, Board of Studies (English), Professor Latha, Ms. Nirmala and Professor G.

Damodar (Rtd.) for their encouragement. My thanks are also due to Professor Raja Gopalachary (Rtd.), Professor P. Mallikarjuna Rao (Rtd.), Professor P. Shailaja (Rtd.) and K. Damodar Rao (Rtd.) for their moral support in the course of my work.

I am indebted to my beloved parents, late Mr. P.R. Devanand and Mrs. Mitilda Eunice, who have been the inspiration for my career development. My thanks are due to my husband Dr. K. Kumara Swamy and my daughters Nidhi Siya, Nikhitha and Nishika for being a constant support. I am also thankful to my brothers P.D. Vinod Paul and P.D. Prabhakar and my sisters Mrs. P.D. Sujatha and P.D. Sabitha, for their cooperation, sustained endurance and assistance.

Warangal **P. BABITHA VIVEKAVATHI**

Introduction

Indian English literature is an important outcome of English education in India under colonial rule. In the recent years, it has initiated widespread interest both in India and abroad. Modern Indian literature is partly the result of the Western breath, having the roots of tradition. Today, fiction has a prominent position in Indian English literature. There are many developments and there is a distinct shift in the nature and study of Indian English fiction. C.N. Srinath rightly says that "Indian fiction has made significant strides" (65).

Today Indian English fiction has become vivid, intricate and rich with themes winning worldwide accolades. In literature, it refers to any mode that approaches a text with foremost concern for the nature of female experience. Postcolonial Indian women writers, intent upon speaking their identity through narrative, find a space for themselves within the postcolonial nation. B.S. Goyal's comment is relevant in this context: "Indo-English literature can be seen as a product of post-Independent India" (98). It no longer limits the writings only for the sons of the soil. Globally it explores the scope of fictional concerns of the writers as purely Indian.

Western modern Education forced new principles of life upon women. Legally, woman has been given equal rights as man. It is a universally acknowledged fact that woman performs on par with man physically and mentally. Women have changed in the society according to the time as they were denied the liberty to express their feelings, thoughts and anguish and had remained inferior to men. They have been working both indoors and outdoors but their services remain unrecognized. Men cannot adjust to the notion of women being equal to man. Though equal opportunities of education and economic independence were provided for women, they remained victims of domestic injustice and were denied legal rights.

In the twentieth century, Indian women novelists started the discourse in English language. Evolving from a representation of their traditional and confined position, their expression has emerged fully liberated and bold in the contemporary era. The resistance to marriage started in the 1980s. R.S. Pathak aptly observes: "It is during the eighties that Indian English novelists and novels earned unheard of honors and distinctions in the Western academic world" (14). Many Indian women novelists of the 1990s wrote novels which explored the true state of Indian society, women's attempt to establish an identity and stop the influence of patriarchal society.

The 21st century novels have changed the face of traditional portrayal of suffering women and have moved towards women exploring their individuality and identity. Pam Morris writes about the role and responsibility of women writers in creating new trends of living: "Creative forms of writing can offer special insights into human experience and sharpen our perception of social reality. Literary texts may therefore provide a more meaningful understanding of the ways in which society works to the disadvantage of women. In addition, the strong emotional impact of imaginative writing may be brought into play to increase indignation at gender discrimination and hence helps to end it. Positive images of female experience and qualities can be used to raise women's self-esteem and lend authority to their political demands" (7).

The distinction between committed and uncommitted writers becomes meaningful only when we examine particular novels. It was in the political struggles against foreign policy that women of all communities and classes began to participate aggressively in life and step out of home, with the support of nationalist political leaders who saw the advantages of mobilizing women. Gandhi was conscious about the authority of non-violent struggle on women and disagreed that they are by nature non-violent and have great skill to abide torment. In an article on Gandhi entitled "Not by Faith Alone," Ramachandra Guha observes: "Gandhi affirmed as early as 1918 that woman has the same right of freedom and liberty. He dismissed the ideas put forward by Manu as an interpolation and if it was not an Interpolation, he could only say that in Manu's days, women did not have the status they deserved" (*Sunday Express* 1st Oct).

The adversaries of women's political participation expressed a number of objections and cautioned against breaking down traditional feminist roles. Some based their disapproval on the religious beliefs. The doings of women in the pre-independence movement transformed the accusation portraying parallels between foreign policy and patriarchal suppression.

Feminist issues outclass all limits of nationality, race, creed, etc., and have been reflecting the feeling of idiosyncrasy and expressing their revolt against the male world. Globally one of the major concerns of the contemporary literature has been to highlight the plight of women, their increasing problems, their physical and economic mistreatment, and their mental torment in the male dominated society in every field of life. The main focus is to bring into light the oppression experienced by women in various forms in all walks of life. Establishment of various women study centres and formation of various welfare organizations are indication of the fact that the voice of women is being heard. In order to reach the stage of being listened to, the women writers struggled through their writing to project their point of view and fight for a change in the attitude of society towards women.

The feminist movement was brought into light by Betty Friedan's *The Feminine Mystique* (1963). She interviewed many wives and mothers and revealed the hollowness of woman's happiness in marriage and motherhood, although they had been blessed with all the comforts of life. They were purely trying to search for fulfilment by playing the role of a devoted wife and caring mother. Friedan writes: "A man has the need for self-fulfilment, autonomy, self-realization, independence, individuality; self-actualization is as important as the sexual need, with as serious consequences when it is thwarted. Women's sexual problems are, in this sense, by-products of the suppression of her basic need to grow and fulfil her potentialities as a human being, potentialities which the mystique of feminism fulfilment ignores" (282).

The second-generation Indian women novelists brought out significant novels from time to time. Kamala Markandaya's contribution by now has been recognized globally. Nayantara Sahgal's *Rich like Us* (1985) made great contribution towards storytelling; Kamala Das's autobiographical works laid the paths hitherto unknown to Indian English novelists.

Kamala Markandaya wrote for the welfare of humanity and alleviation of human suffering. Her novels take us to the heart of a South Indian village where life has not changed for centuries. Her writing presents the unique female perspective. *Nectar in a Sieve* portrays the obstacles faced by women in Hindu orthodox household. Her writing can also be viewed in terms of women's psyche which is rooted in class, race, nationality and history.

Markandaya gives realistic and human touch to woman's struggle to find happiness in a changing India. The novel underscores the rampant hunger and indebtedness of the Indian peasant. Rukmani is 'the central consciousness,' as Henry James termed it, through which the events come filtered to the readers. Rukmani's tale could be any village woman's tale in India of the nineteen fifties. Her family life was peaceful with her simple joys and sorrows. She was proud of the love and care of her husband. She needed nothing else—no wealth, no luxury and no material pleasure. But Rukmani's serene life is disturbed as she fails to give birth to a son. Later, she gets a number of sons through the help of Dr. Kenny. Ira, daughter of Rukmani, is abandoned by her husband as she remains childless even after five years of her marriage. Ira takes to prostitution to save the family from starvation. The socio-economic conditions affect Rukmani and her daughter Ira.

The novel reveals that fear, hunger, and despair are the companions of the peasant. Srinivasa Iyengar opines: "fear of the dark future; fear of the sharpness of hunger; fear of blackness of death" (483). Rukmani is the binding force in the family. Her values are to be redefined in a chaotic world of conflicting. Parvati Bhatnagar aptly remarks: "Values need to be redefined, so also human relationship, especially within the family. Such is the dilemma of the middle class. An adherence to the traditional values has become difficult. New values have yet to be evolved. It requires tremendous courage and thoughtlessness to break, away from the tradition" (50-57).

Markandaya's second novel *Some Inner Fury* is about Premala who is from a conservative Hindu family. She sacrifices everything only to find her husband's home and his English friends disgusting. She tries to seek relief by helping Hickey, an English missionary, to run a school for the village boys. Markandaya through Premala shows the traditional Indian woman encountering a culture in transition.

Sarojini, the protagonist in Markandaya's third novel *Silence of Desire* (1961), overcomes her problems through god-fearing nature and spirituality. Her religious beliefs and her visits to Swami to get her tumour cured, irritate her husband. Fifteen years of her married life are disturbed until Swami leaves the place and asks her to undergo the operation for her tumour. In this novel, Markandaya portrays the complexity of man-woman relationship.

Mahashweta Devi's stories show how the elite culture of nationalism excludes the subaltern. In *Stanadayini* [breast-giver], the maternal figure becomes a critique of the nation construct. Jashoda, the lactating and bounteous woman, becomes a wet-nurse in the Haldar household to support her impoverished family. The motherly figure is seen more in terms of function than as an individual. She is left to die a slow and painful death. There is a continuous reference to the female body as an object of the male gaze and as a means of procreation.

Women are presented as chaste and unblemished by Bhabani Bhattacharya. These women are pure but their energetic vitality is crushed, and they are invariably victimized. In his novel *So Many Hungers* (1947), Bhabani Bhattacharya projects a grim picture of the uprooted families of the villagers during the Bengal famine. The young women are raped and inducted into brothels of Calcutta for a few rupees. Santosh Gupta points out: "women writers have eloquently voiced women side of life, the experiences of man's 'other,' society's marginalized and silenced half, breaking off from the traditional male-dominated novels that focussed on public subjects and public space, women novels have brought to centre-stage the ignored and unexpressed lives that have been on the periphery of male lives" (23).

Bharati Mukherjee's novels articulate the protagonists' experience of the Indian traditions, and the conflict with western attitudes. Her novels are the outcome of the cultural alienation that is a world phenomenon. Her novel *Wife* is the story of Amit and his wife Dimple, newly-married immigrants to the U.S.A. Amit and Dimple leave their country in search of their dreams. Dimple is a naive girl who thinks that her wedding would bring freedom and love.

Their migration or "cultural transplant" leads not only to a crisis of identity but greatly affects their personal relationship. While Dimple tries to mould herself as a responsible wife, Amit is not satisfied and develops a feeling that he is not the man of her dreams. Dimple's ill-conceived compulsions are precipitated by the violence-ridden individualistic American life which culminates in her killing of her husband. She is unable to come to terms with either her own or America's culture and, almost in a fit of hallucination, kills her husband. Bharati Mukherjee experiments with the complexity of inner experience of her protagonist which comes as a shock to man-wife relationship in the modern times.

Anita Desai's famous novels *Cry the Peacock* (1963), *Voices in the City* (1965), *Bye-Bye Blackbird* (1971), *Where Shall We Go This Summer* (1975), *Fire on the Mountain* (1977), *Clear Light of Day* (1980) and *The Village by The Sea* (1982) graphically present the chaotic psyche of the modern woman. Her heroines are intelligent and sensible, but in an attempt to manage home and children and accomplish emotional fulfilment, they reach the threshold of mental crisis.

Cry the Peacock, Anita Desai's first novel, reveals the gloomy psychological battle in the mind of Maya, a young girl worried about the disastrous predictions in her childhood. Maya's father marries her off to his lawyer friend Gautama without considering the age gap between his friend and her daughter. Maya longed for her husband's attention which collided with the extremely practical outlook of her husband. She is portrayed as a tormented soul who is still childish and shows little inclination to take up the adult responsibilities. Maya is like a trapped bird as she cannot escape from her present. The inability to bear a child adds to her misery. Gautama is down-to-earth, unromantic, and cynical, believes in 'detachment' on every count. Maya is a talented and sensitive woman, gifted with poetic imagination. Maya's grief at the loss of her pet dog matters little to Gautama.

Gautama is killed by Maya, turning her into a psychopath. Her depression brings to limelight the modern existential predicament. Shyam M. Asnani writes that concept of free woman "transcends the limits of economic or social freedom and becomes a mental or emotional attitude." (66) Anita Desai explored the inner sensibility in her novels and added a new facet to the success of Indian women writers in English fiction.

Kiran Desai, a diasporic writer, received accolades for her first novel *Hullabaloo in the Guava Orchard* (1998). She won Betti Trask Award—a prize given by the society of Authors for the best new novels by citizens of the Commonwealth Nations. Her second novel *The Inheritance of Loss* (2006) fetched her

Booker's Prize as well as the 2006 National Book Critics Circle Fiction Award. About *The Inheritance of Loss*, Santan writes: "Kiran Desai highlights that the process of globalization has its loopholes, that the cartographical binaries have collapsed only for a blessed few. The poor people of the third world countries who dream of a better future and are lured by the affluence of the American society have no place in the world of their dream" (87).

Namita Gokhale has written five novels: *Paro: Dreams of Passion* (1984), *Gods, Graves and Grandmother* (1994), *A Himalayan Love Story* (1996), *The Book of Shadows* (1999) and *Shakuntala* (2005). Her non-fiction works are *Mountain Echoes: Reminiscence and Kumaoni Woman* (1994), *The Book of Shiva* (2000), *Love Them, Loathe Them* (2004), *Present Tense, Living on the Edge* (2004), and *The Puffen Mahabharata* (2009). Her works deal with unrequited love, passion and jealousies.

Uma Vasudev is a writer of rare talent. She wrote many short stories that have appeared in *Short Stories International*, New York. She is also editor of *Surge International*, a political and cultural magazine from New Delhi. A passionate storyteller, Uma Vasudev portrays the rapture and torment of a man who is lust-stricken. After many years he learns how his existence has turned futile with a loveless sex but later realize the importance of love. Her feministic view created uproar in Indian circles and is depicted well in her novel *The Song of Anasuya* and short stories.

Anita Rau Badami is an Indian Canadian novelist. Her first novel *Tamarind Man* (1997) was her thesis for a course on Creative Writing. Her novels deal with the entanglement of Indian life and cultural gap that emerges when Indians move to the West. Her other novels are: The *Hero's Walk* (2001), *Can You Hear the Nightbird Call?* (2006). She expresses the anguish of Indian immigrants. "In this globalized mess of categories, Badami's response is remarkably clear. She defines herself primarily as a writer and doesn't feel the compulsion to identify herself with any one community." (55)

Shoba De is another popular fiction writer. She is the first Indian woman writer who explores the world of urban women in India. De's novels and essays are a creative endeavour to shatter patriarchal hegemony. She became popular after the publication of the bestseller *Socialite Evenings*. De's novels reveal her intimate understanding of the psyche of women. Shobha De's explosive novel *Strange Obsession* revolves around the life and lustful relationship of two young women Amrita and Meenakshi. Fundamentally, it seems to be a psychosomatic sexual obsession of strange woman Meenakshi, also known as Minx.

In *Starry Nights* (1992), the mother of a popular film star and her three daughters deserted by their husbands live with another woman. The mother forces her twelve-year-old daughter to work in the blue films to get some money to run the house and pay for children's fees. At the age of fifteen, the mother makes her go to bed with every Tom, Dick, and Harry in the film industry of Bombay to make her a film star but the daughter is sad and morose every time she faces sexual assaults. Madhu Jain says: "The *Starry Nights* is described as 'confession of man-eater'" (195). Shobha De moves away from the beaten path and undertakes a serious analysis of the man-woman relationship.

Nayantara Sahgal is the leading practitioner of the political novel in India. Her first five novels have a political event as the background. *Rich Like Us* (1985) is Sahgal's best novel which she wrote in the United States on a Woodrow Wilson Fellowship. The novel presents a picture of India of 1975-1976, the time her cousin Indira Gandhi declared National Emergency and assumed absolute power for about twenty months.

Sahgal's themes are politics (her natural material), freedom (both in its public and individual sense) and Hinduism. Her novels reflect the consciousness with sudden and strange change in which the individual character and the annoyance of collective life is shaped. She says that marriage is a sacred institution and not just a sexual relationship. She depicts with keen insight and sensitivity the problems and suffering of women in marriage. The novel *Rich like Us* revolves round the young Sonali who works in the ministry as a joint secretary. Sonali is unaware of the prime minister's younger son's business of manufacturing indigenous car and the secret deal between the foreign businessman and his Indian associate regarding starting a factory of fizzy drink. Sonali finds the file to be insignificant, unfair and waste of foreign exchange and so writes an unfavourable note but did not know that the project was tip of an iceberg, and was a cover-up to store imported car parts. She is transferred to her home state to a lower position for writing an unfavourable note. Ravi Kachru, an old friend of Sonali, takes over as joint secretary. He establishes the factory quickly but simultaneously gets into trouble for not paying the Indian and foreign money to the minister who receives it through his daughter-in-law. Dev is the son of an old prosperous businessman who is totally paralyzed; Dev is shattered completely by his shady business and for withdrawing the huge amount of money from his father's account forging the paralyzed father's signature.

Finally, the loser is Dev's stepmother and Sonali's aunt Rose who is under stress about her future. She meets an accidental death of drowning herself in a well which is officially considered a suicide by the young wing of the government party. The British couple which has come to see Sonali's paralysed uncle Ravi picks Sonali which finally changes her pathetic situation and allows her to concentrate in the medieval India's decorative arts.

Ruth Prawer Jhabvala deals with the problems faced by women who are influenced by western culture. In her first novel *To Whom She Will*, the protagonist Amrita flirts with Hari Shahni who is traditional in his attitude but finally marries a bachelor selected by her parents. Similarly in *Nature of Passion*, Nimmy has western attitude, but marries Kallu, a boy who belongs to her religion and community instead of marrying Pheroze. Jhabvala, no doubt, presents a Sati-Savitri archetype image of woman who is devoted to her husband. She has also described women who have guts to go against the will of their husbands by leading a separated life. Sarla Devi and Gulab are women who desert their husbands because they are immoral and irresponsible towards them.

Arundhati Roy is a talented and committed writer. Her novel *The God of Small Things* fetched her the Booker Prize. She questions the power politics and attempts a kind of reform through the power embodied in the art of storytelling. She exposes Indian social structure—class and caste ridden Indian society. *God of Small Things* talks about various hierarchies on which Indian society is structured and acknowledges the condition of the nation around us without any distortion or aberration. It is clear that Roy does not retain an unmistakably national pride in her country. She allows herself to support a redefined nationalism. Her political activism suggests that the nation can be mobilized on behalf of minority groups, including women groups disadvantaged both by tradition and by the trans-nationalism associated with globalized capital. Bimaljit writes: "Arundhati Roy's novel *The God of Small Things* unfurls a plethora of details regarding the changing political scene in Kerala, the problems besetting women in a male-dominated society, caste taboos, the lives of rudderless children of a broken home, and in the main, vivid description of bees and birds, flowers and trees, sky and river, in a language that is immensely captivating." (95)

Manju Kapur's semi-autobiographical novel *Difficult Daughters* is about female oppression and male-chauvinism. The protagonist's struggle for career and identity against the leading beliefs of domesticity is set around the turbulent years of World War II and the partition of India. Manju Kapur depicts women of three generations: Kasturi, the mother, Virmati, the difficult daughter, and Ida, Virmati's daughter. Focusing on Virmati, the novel brings to light India's fight for freedom from the British Raj.

Virmati fights for the freedom to live life on her terms. Virmati's mother is depicted in the conventional mould. Her father is a benevolent patriarch. In this novel, patriarchy works in a different manner; it deals with the divergence between the traditional and the modern. Virmati is unlike her mother Kasturi who surrenders to the patriarchal society. She tries to suppress Virmati's desire for emancipation but Virmati rebels against the patriarchal norms.

Virmati is brought up in a family where the woman has no identity of her own, no right for higher education. Born in an austere family with a doughty courage, she challenges the authority of her parents and family to acquire a higher academic degree in life. She rebels and prepares to sacrifice her family and all norms of male-dominated society to continue her higher studies.

Kapur portrays a conventional family that considers a woman's education secondary, while giving importance to marriage and family duties as her primary objectives. Virmati is torn between family liability, the desire for education and unlawful love affair. She rebels and her decision to marry Harish, an already married man, is a clear defiance of the conventions of the society to which she belongs. Dipika Sahai writes: "Her self-assertion goes to the extent of having illicit love with the married Professor whom she subsequently marries. The hardship and suffering involved in fighting against an established order, the shattering experience of rejection by her family on becoming the second wife of the professor, and the resultant alienation from society forms the theme of the novel. Her life is a continuous struggle. She wants to establish an order through defiance. She rebels against the accepted and existing moral codes and social norms." (8-12)

Virmati feels she is entrapped by the strong bars of traditional patriarchal norms. The novelist projects her protagonist as a woman wedged between the passion of the physical appearances and yearning to be part of political and intellectual movements.

Manju Kapur's second novel *A Married Woman* was published in 2002. It was shortlisted for the Society of Authors 2004 Encore Award for the best second book. *A Married Woman* is a seductive lesbian love story, set at a time of political and religious turmoil. The destruction of the Babri Mosque parallels Astha's emotional turmoil, a story told with sympathy and intelligence. Manju Kapur depicts the political situation with enthusiasm: "Her parents take utmost interest in her and want to see her do well in her studies, for the eligibility level of the marriage. They give her emancipation but she exploits the emancipation given by her parents which leads to an affair with Bunty and then with Rohan. Later her marriage with Hemant smoothens through conjugal bliss, but slowly she feels alienation and dissatisfaction with her married life. Manju Kapur has delineated Astha's character as a woman who asks a bit more of life than tradition will automatically give her" (Verma 55).

After marriage, everything changes. Astha's husband Hemant is busy with his business and has little time to share her feelings and daily routine matters. She feels lonely at home and her loneliness drives her to take up the profession of teaching. She develops friendship with Aijaz, a political street theatre actor and a History teacher who comes to teach at the same school. Their friendship does not last long as he dies during an agitation. After Aijaz's death, Astha develops an affair with Aijaz wife Pipeelika who offers her much comfort. Their relationship grows and the two women become intense lovers. Manju Kapur writes about the relationship of Astha and Pipee in an interview and says: "An affair with a man would have been the classic cliché and so I ruled it out and tried out a same sex affair. I don't know how successful I have been nor is this based on any real-life relationship. It is as I said a writer's experiment with a plot." (Web 2012)

Astha now has to choose between her stay with the tradition and safety of her home and children, or make a run for her emancipation and a lesbian love affair. The book ends on a note of compromise as the two women realize that they do not have a future together.

Home, Manju Kapur's third novel, is a pure narrative with vivid characters that are introduced with details of an ordinary middle-class family which unravels the life story of a joint family in Delhi. It brings to light the still prevalent narrow-minded attitudes of bringing up a girl child. It is the story of two Meerut-born sisters, Sona and Rupa. Rupa marries a junior government officer and lives modestly while Sona enjoys all the comforts provided by the extended family business. Sona is an independent woman in a nuclear family who emerges with her pickle business without any trauma of her childlessness.

In Indian families, life is based on a woman's ability to bear a male child. The daughter-in-law in the family finds her status judged according to the child she bears and the ability to give a male heir to the family. Shamed by years of barrenness, Sona finally is blessed with a girl Nisha and boy Raju. Nisha shows signs of emotional distress at the trauma of secret sexual abuse, she grows up under the care of her aunt Rupa. Nisha grows up to revolt. The novel then focuses on her failed college romance, the growth of poor skin condition, delayed marriage and desperate loneliness that triggers her venture into entrepreneurship. Later, she suffers from the pressures of marriage and motherhood.

Manju Kapur is aware of the petty jealousies, insecurities and compulsions that play a major part in the joint-family set up. She is conscious of the complex mental make-up of her women characters. She explores many unsaid emotions that they experience.

The fourth novel *Immigrant* is the story of Delhi-based Nina Batra, a thirty-year-old unmarried lecturer. The death of her father has left Nina and her mother struggle to make the two ends meet. The novel begins on Nina's thirtieth birthday which fills the gloomy thoughts of delayed marriage. Soon her family is introduced to an NRI dentist groom Anand and the marriage takes place. After the marriage, Nina leaves her job in India and goes to Canada along with Anand. She faces many problems of adjustment in the foreign country and to find a good job. She has a psychological conflict as she tries to adapt to the western way of life and culture: "Underneath the emancipation, the western woman may not be better off than her sisters elsewhere; we have privileges that make it harder to uncover our inner servitude, without awareness we can be both—manipulated and manipulative, exploited as well as exploitative" (192).

The man-woman relationship is woven around the immigration. Anand goes through a long therapy for the sexual problem which he hides from Nina. He feels embarrassed to share his problem with her. Nina feels cheated and betrayed when she comes to know about the therapy. Nina then joins the library science course to divert her mind but gets into an extra-marital affair. However, she soon realizes her inability to adapt to a sudden cultural change and begins to dislike the barren relationship. She feels rootless in the foreign land and finally overcomes the feeling by increasing her personal value in the form of excellent academic record, encouraging attitudes and confidence.

Manju Kapur's fifth novel *Custody* is set in the upper-middle class colonies of Delhi in the mid-nineties. It depicts modern marriages heavy with the woman's thirst for individualism and independence. It deals with the lives of two women, Shagun and Ishita, where one fights to move away from her husband and the other to join her husband.

Shagun, the blue-eyed stunning beauty, is wife of Raman, an intelligent and enterprising middle-class aspirant with IIT and IIM degrees, blessed with two beautiful children Arjun and Roohi. Her marital life changes when she meets her husband's boss, Ashok Khanna. Shagun and Ashok are attracted towards each other and have an extra-marital affair which leads to Shagun's filing a divorce case. Their marriage is fractured and the children suffer. Ashok is ready to take up the role of the father for the two biological children of Shagun and Raman. However as per the court's verdict, the boy Arjun stays in the custody of his mother, while Raman takes care of girl Roohi.

Ishita, the wife of Suryakanta, is a loving wife and devoted daughter-in-law who earns the goodwill of the family members.

But everything changes as months pass without any news of pregnancy. Fate brings Ishita and Raman together. The lonely man and the destitute woman join to make a new family. Ishita shows true love and care towards Roohi, her only child now. The novel reveals the unimagined uncertainties of matrimony. Finally, the separated couples are happy with their crisscross wives, leaving behind their husbands.

The role of women has significantly altered in the postcolonial era; they have control on their bodies and decisions. Manju Kapur makes a strong impact by depicting the changing face of Indian women who suffer but are stoic. They break through traditional boundaries to carve a niche for themselves. The maturity of the adolescent mind is well experimented in the life of her heroines.

Manju Kapur's sixth novel is *Brothers*; it is about the women who are unidentified and serve silently their family. It highlights the lives of women in multiple locations, rural, urban, domestic and public. They contribute to the happenings in the home and the outside world. The story has the span of eight decades, from World War II to the first decade of the 21st century and mirrors the plot of the actual event which took place in 2006. The novel starts with the assassination of Himmat Singh Gaina, chief minister of the province of Rajasthan, by his younger brother Mangal; they are the sons of Dhanpal Giana of Lalbanga village.

The novel begins in the ancestral village of Lalbanga. The story depicts uncle Virpal, who leaves his village and goes to Ajmer to join Gandhi in the protest against British rule. Eventually he co-founds the Indian Progressive People's Party (IPPP), "with its roots in Hindu culture and identity." Virpal's brother, Dhanpal, in stark contrast, joins the British army to fight the Germans in Africa. When he hears about Dhanpal's enrolling, Virpal returns to his village as a rich man, no longer a farmer but a businessman with political aspirations.

Tapti, the wife of Mangal and the lover of Himmat, cries more over Himmat's death than for her jailed husband Mangal. Tapti makes choices that aren't allowed to other women characters. She does not yield to having more children. The traditional family considers women as property and child-producing machines. But Tapti fulfils her desire to work and earn for herself and her daughters. Her husband neither supports nor suppresses her decisions.

Tapti rises above the rest as an educated woman with unwavering ambition to fulfil her desire. The depiction of the human struggle, ambition and raw emotions is compelling. The book delves deep into the ways in which the modern, city-bred sense of equality leads to tension in the married life. Manju Kapur writes that the angan or the kitchen is a place where the women share their distress and find comfort, through gestures or with few words. The potency of the book lies in its aptitude to mock at the strands of ancestral relationships and the moral complexities of multiple attachments, setting them against the backdrop of changes wrought by politics and time.

Jai Nimbkar has written about a variety of themes and problems concerning the Indian woman, particularly in the socio-economic context of the post-Independence India. Inequality of sexes, place of woman in her family and society, her search for personal identity, the meaning of marriage and its effect on the woman are some of the major thematic concerns of Jai Nimbkar's fiction. The author meticulously deals with the theme of marriage in Indian context in her three novels.

Temporary Answers is her first full-length novel which deals with human relationships through the life of the protagonist Vineeta. The sudden death of her husband forces Vineeta, a pediatrician, to face the conflicts as a widow. Vilas, her childhood friend, helps her to start a practice as a doctor and intends to marry her. Vineeta rejects him as he treats her as a fragile woman. She falls in love with Abhijit who is a college lecturer and playwright, but their association leaves her only with a temporary answer. They love each other but he distances himself from her because of his interest in writing plays and spends time alone. He feels their relationship may hamper his work and tries to avoid her. Vineeta is surprised by his attitude and decides to stay only as a friend.

Vineeta boldly takes the decision to stay as widow instead of getting into the bond of marriage. She feels that there should be respect and understanding between the couple. She feels marriage and love are all only temporary answers to avoid loneliness. She experiences three distinct relationships, with her husband Nagendra, her childhood friend Vilas and her lover Abhijit. Vineeta aspires to get something unique from her life and succeeds in realizing her identity. She comes to the conclusion that marriage is only a temporary answer and not a final solution to women's problems

Jai Nimbkar's second novel entitled *A Joint Venture* was published in 1988, fourteen years after the publication of her first novel. Nimbkar delves deep into male chauvinistic society and presents an authentic conflict between tradition and postmodernity. The middle-class married woman's identity crisis emerges from her works. *A Joint Venture* comes close to being, as per the claim on its cover, "A truly mature novel by the author of *Temporary Answers*." The novel explores the suffering and emancipation of the career woman.

The protagonist Jyoti Deshmukh's married life of thirty years which is compressed with remarkable brevity. The novel opens with the startling decision of Jyoti to leave her husband Ram after thirty years. Unable to understand her decision, Ram advises Jyoti to think about it again and quickly plans a holiday at their favourite hill resort. Ram feels that spending time together at Mahabaleshwar will calm her down and make her change her decision. The novel unfolds thirty years of her married life in a series of flashbacks.

Jyoti is happy after her marriage as Ram is from a rich family while she comes from a poor middle-class family. She moulds herself at her in-laws' place in a village, though she's from the city. She takes care of the farming, monitors the work of the women who come to work at their farm. The problem starts when Ram starts Seeds Business with the help of Jyoti. As business expands, Ram spends most of his time in the business and has less time for the wife and children. Jyoti is worried about the children and Ram's too much involvement in business. He does not share anything with her and takes decision independently. Though Jyoti does most of the work in business, she gets least importance.

The differences arise when Ram starts partying with rich people. Jyoti condemns his association with them but he does not listen. She feels neglected and decides to leave. She meets her friend Vinnie and shares that she has left Ram because of the problems she was facing. Vinnie is surprised to learn about Jyoti's decision. She later informs her that their business has suffered heavy loss as Ram has been cheated by his counterpart who put Triveni Seed labels on adulterated seeds. Learning about the situation, Jyoti goes back to him. The novel ends with reunion of Jyoti and Ram.

Jai Nimbkar's third novel *Come Rain* depicts the cross-cultural conflict. The protagonist is a young American girl Ann, idealistic and freedom loving, who falls in love with the Indian traditions and values and marries Ravi, an orthodox Hindu boy from Pune. She comes to India with her husband. Ravi cannot help constantly comparing India's poverty and dirt with the affluence of America. He looks down upon the Indian culture and social ethos. On the other hand, Ann adopts the Indian milieu as her own, without giving up her own American values.

Jhumpa Lahiri in her debut novel *Namesake* (2003) weaves a story covering three decades of the Ganguli household in the USA. An incident of train accident becomes the leitmotif. The naming of his son as Gogol and later as Nikhil brings in a conflict between the two names and identities. It is not only a way of knowing oneself but also how one perceives oneself and how others perceive you. Lahiri underlines the efforts required to mediate between people and situations as also between cultures and social practices.

Githa Hariharan, the distinguished recipient of the prestigious commonwealth award, published her novel *The Thousand Faces of Night* in1992. Her women are not bothered by traditional middle-class attitudes, views, opinions, and taboos, which condemn them to live within the four walls of their homes.

The novelist depicts the protagonist Devi's life and her shattering dreams. Devi marries Mahesh, a regional manager, who treats her as an object to satisfy his sexual urge. He has no regard for her emotions and fails to become a reliable husband. She feels quite insecure as the sense of loneliness creeps into her life. She moves towards Gopal, a man of music, warmth and affection, after the failure of her relationship with her husband. However, her relationship with Gopal is short-lived. She realizes that both Mahesh and Gopal need women only for sexual satisfaction. She deserts Gopal and begins to live with a widow. She ultimately learns that men do not try to understand emotions of women.

Shashi Deshpande is one of the most prolific contemporary Indian women writers in English. She was born in Dharwad, Karnataka, in 1938. She is the second daughter of the famous dramatist, Sri Ranga. She had English education at a protestant mission school in Karnataka. She graduated in Economics from Bombay and got a gold medal in Law. Later, she took postgraduate degree in English Literature from Mysore university. She devoted her life to bringing up her two sons and later took a course in Journalism. She worked for *Onlooker* magazine for a couple of months and published her first short story in 1970. She has a number of short stories, four children's books and several essays to her credit.

Many of her stories were published in reputed magazines like *Femina* and *Eve's Weekly*. In 1978, she published *Legacy*, the first collection of her short stories. Her other collections of stories are: *It Was Dark, The Miracle* and *It Was the Nightingale*. She also tried her hand at detective writing and wrote three detective serials, two of which were later expanded and published as regular novels, *Come up and Be Dead* and *If I Die Today*. The racy style of writing brought these books popularity but Deshpande herself considers them failures. An early short story, "A Liberated Woman," is about a young woman who marries a man of her choice from different caste in spite of parental opposition. She becomes a successful doctor with her intelligence and hard work but her marriage breaks up because of her achievement.

Shashi Deshpande's *The Legacy* was prescribed for the graduate students in Columbia University. *The Legacy* doesn't have anything exciting or exotic about India—any Maharajahs or snake charmers. The woman deprived of love, understanding and companionship is the centre of her work.

The Intrusion and Other Stories explores the sexual vulnerability of woman and her exploitation as a sex object, which is sanctioned by marriage. On her honeymoon, a young girl is apprehensive of the sex act and her husband's advances. Her husband establishes his superior position in the relationship right in the beginning, humiliating and treating her like an inanimate object. She had been provided to him for his exclusive use through the legal channel of marriage. So, he forces himself upon her brutally while she is asleep.

She wrote ten novels: *The Dark Holds No Terrors* (1980), *If I Die Today* (1982), *Come up and Be Dead* (1983), *That Long Silence* (1988), *The Binding Vine* (1993), *A Matter of Time* (1996), *Small Remedies* (2000), *Moving On* (2004) and *In the Country of Deceit*. *A Matter of Time* was her first work to be published in USA by The Feminist Press of New York in June 1999. She is the winner of the Sahitya Akademi, the Padma Shri (2009) and the Nanjangud Thirumalamba awards. Presently, she lives in Bangalore with her pathologist husband.

Shashi Deshpande is tuned to ordinary experience, vibrantly rendering the ordinary with intelligence, learning and insight. Since her fiction is woman-centred, the "feminine consciousness" becomes the protagonist in her novels. She mixes humanism and feminism in her fiction. Her feminism is not west-oriented because it is born out of a typically Indian situation. She visualizes Indian woman as optimistic and radical. In fact, she would like to call herself a "humanist feminist."

Most of her novels depict women playing the role of daughter, mother and wife. The protagonists find themselves enclosed in a tradition-bound male-oriented society and suffer from loneliness and a sense of a guilt and failure. Her novels and short stories depict social reality. The use of the first-person narrator gives authenticity to the situations and brings the protagonist closer to the reader. She portrays marriage as a social institution, culturally and socially approved relationship between a man and woman that legitimizes a sexual and economic union where individuals make commitment to one another.

Shashi Deshpande focuses on the society's attachment to marriage in her fiction. It is a long-drawn-out drama of negotiation in which she feels uncertain and humiliated. In the fiction of earlier writers, a girl marriage is a *cul-de-sac* making her so dependent. Marriage, which is considered a sacred tie of two souls, is thus desecrated to an extent that it becomes nothing but carnal, involving no responsibility, sharing and understanding of the two minds. But at the same time, she reflects the inability to reject her cultural, social background totally and hence fails to transcend the horizons depicting a revolutionary spirit.

In *Roots and Shadows,* Deshpande's concern with the social and cultural construction of gender, her open protest against the treatment of women as sexual object, her defiance of the stereotyped roles assigned to women, her bold effort to project the prejudiced attitude of the society towards women are obvious. She articulates not only a thematic and technical maturity but also effectively communicates an intense feminine sensibility.

Indu in *Roots and Shadows*, Jaya in *That Long Silence* and Saru in *The Dark Holds No Terrors* are torn between self-expression and social stigmas, material and psychological. They finally succeed in overcoming social stigmas and assert their individuality and realize their potential in the professional arena. Shashi Deshpande's career protagonists are not satisfied with the rhetoric of equality between men and women but want to see that the right to an individual life and the right to development of their individual capabilities are realized in their own lives. The true position of woman in Indian society would emerge by critically examining the relationship with the husband. In a talk Lakshmi Holmstrom questions Shashi Deshpande: "Novels contain so much that is the material of feminist thought: women's sexuality, the construction of gender roles as wives and mother, self-discoveries. To what extent would you call yourself a feminist?" Deshpande replies: "I now have no doubts at all in saying that I am a feminist. In my own life, but not consciously, as a novelist I must also say that my feminism has come to me very slowly, very gradually, and mainly out of my own thinking and experiences and feelings" (22-27).

She cites Betty Friedan and Virginia Woolf in her narrative, and in a subtle way brings into focus feminist issues of identity, selfhood, and autonomy, of bonding and its disruption. Referring to Friedan, she says, "it was easier for her to start the women's lib movement than to change her own personal life" (105).

Shevanthi Bai is a champion of feminism. She combats injustice and ill treatment meted out to simple sober, unsophisticated housewives. She focuses particularly on the tragedy of unsuccessful marital life and widowhood. She advocates freedom, liberty and emancipation of women in order to extricate them from obsequious servitude and in human torture to which they were subjected by their husbands, mother-in-law and others. Her novel *Ratnabai* has a feminist perspective. She portrays the agony of the girl Ratnabai who is persecuted by the relatives of her father-in-law for going to school for higher education. The novel voices the need of education for women.

Another woman novelist of the pre-Independence India was Sorabji a feminist and a social reformer. As an advocate by profession, she deals with the cause of women and shows the mental agony of married and unmarried women, widows and victims of child marriage. *Love and Life behind the Purdah* (1901) *Sun Babies* (1904) and *Between the Twilights* (1908) are the stories that focus realistically on the inner mind of the suppressed women living behind purdah. The first one is a collection of ten stories, each seeking to evoke sympathy for the socially and sexually tortured women who dare not raise their voice for deliverance from persecution. These stories explore into the deeper mindset, that reacts passively and timidly to various forms of oppression.

Swarna Kumari Ghosal is different from contemporary women novelists in the choice of themes for her fiction. Her novels *The Fatal Garland* (1910) and *An Unfinished Son* (1913) are historical romances that deal with the theme of love rather than the tragic life of fettered women. Ghosal is not concerned with the psychological suffering of Indian women behind purdah. She seems to have fallen back upon the traditional Victorian device of exploiting the theme of love and romance.

Jane Austen, who upholds the feminist approach in her novels, depicts only the problems of marriageable girls looking for worthy husbands of their choice. The themes of her six novels are identical: the search of the mothers or aunts for grooms for their daughters and nieces. All events in her novels centre round the affairs of love, engagements, festivities, picnics, frustration and disappointment in marital life. Her characters in their state of disappointment never undergo deep psychological agony, which the Indian women experience in their male-dominated families. Jane Austen presents the English women from a feminist viewpoint.

The first novel of Chitra Banerjee Divakaruni is *The Mistress of Spices* (1997) which is set in the United States. The protagonist Tilottama serves the immigrants through her Indian cuisine. She also helps the immigrants to overcome homesickness with her service. Commenting on the works of the novelist, Krishnaiah says: "Her works present mysticism, emotional completeness and reconciliation of the multifarious issues involved in the life of immigrants. She re-evaluates her homeland's culture, concentrating on the status of women and unfolding its ancient myths and ethnicities." (59)

Divakaruni's *Sisters of My Heart* (1999) shows the complex relationships in Chatterjee family of Bengal. Their ancestral properties come down as they are left only with girls, mother and aunts. Sudha and Anju are distant cousins who lose their fathers, and they start facing hurdles in their life due to their innocence. They together share their problems and worries but their association leaves them only with tragedies and betrayals.

Arranged Marriage (1995) is Divakaruni's collection of eleven short stories. Women in these stories struggle with fear and chaos. Her work *The Unknown Errors of Our Lives* (2001) is a volume of nine stories which deals with the characters from South Asian suburbs of U.S.A. Somdatta Mandal opines that the stories mirror "how the changing times are affecting the cherished Indian Institution of arranged marriage" (164).

Women who constitute half the world's population are strangely enough not treated on par with men in all spheres of human activity. They are oppressed, suppressed and discriminated against in all walks of life, despite the fact that every woman is the backbone of her family, her husband and children. The picture of suppressed woman is not something unique to India; it is the predicament of women all over the world. Ernestine observes: "Humanity recognizes no sex, mind recognizes no sex; life and death, pleasure and pain, happiness and misery recognize no sex. Like man, woman comes involuntarily into existence; like him, she possesses physical and mental and moral powers . . . like him she has to pay the penalty for disobeying nature's laws, and far greater penalties she has to suffer from ignorance . . . like men she also enjoys or suffers with her country. Yet she is not recognized as his equal!" (1)

Virginia Woolf's A *Room of One's Own* came out with a detailed program for the emancipation of woman. The industrial revolution showed woman's capacity to do hard manual work. It also paved way for the leftist movements and incorporated the liberation of women. Virginia Woolf opines that there is a need for woman's economic independence and privacy in the house so that she may be able to think and write what she likes.

Simone De Beauvoir came out with a bold manifesto for attacking the patriarchal hegemony in society. In her famous treatise *The Second Sex*, she, like a raging rebel, hits hard at the androcentric customs and conventions, art and culture, philosophy and religion which have assigned the woman a secondary role. She says that man considers himself to be the subject while woman is considered the 'other.' Beauvoir writes about the institution of marriage: "This results in making marriage a union freely entered into by two independent persons whose obligation as contracting parties are personal and reciprocal. Due to contraceptive technology, the reproductive function has ceased to be merely a natural servitude; it is now becoming compatible with productive labour. Another result is that male guardianship of woman is disappearing. With all the developments, de Beauvoir prefers to call our epoch, from the feminist point of view, a period of transition, since only a part of the female population is engaged in production and even they belong to a society in which traditional values are dominant." (445)

Although the critics have studied Indian English fiction from the perspectives of liberation of woman, quest for identity, cross-cultural conflict, self-realization, existentialism, alienation, feminism, gender discrimination and man-woman relationship, not much work has been done to focus on the emancipation of women in the novels of Manju Kapur and Jai Nimbkar. The present study is an attempt in this direction.

Some critics have written articles on Manju Kapur's novels. Ahmad Nadia studies Manju Kapur's *Difficult Daughters* from the perspective of tradition versus modernity and feminism, realism, narrative technique, characterization, images and symbols. Chitralekha Basu discusses Manju Kapur's A *Married Women* from the perspective of Feminism. B.R. Agarwal examines Manju Kapur's *Difficult Daughters* exploring the crisis in value system. Devika finds disastrous synthesis of desire and duty in Virmati, the protagonist in *Difficult Daughters.* Arpita Ghosh studies Manju Kapur's *Difficult Daughters* from the perspective of the plight of women. Seema Malik analyses *Difficult Daughters* from the perspective of women crossing the patriarchal threshold. J.V.N.L. Mythili finds conflict and modernity in Virmati's life. Kalpana Rajput examines the self syndrome in the novels of Manju Kapur. Samuel P. and Shankar discuss human relationships depicted in Manju Kapur *Difficult Daughters.*

P.G. Joshi discusses women empowerment and postcolonial discourse in her novels. R.K. Sharma finds in the novel a presentation of new woman's transformation. Bijay Kumar Das finds character progression in the novel. Ramesh Kumar Gupta holds Jaya a traditional woman, the embodiment of tolerance who changes into modern egotistical self-assertive rebellious woman. Sunita Agarwal focuses on the feministic perspective of *A Married Woman* and explores space and opportunity needed in both economic and social spheres. Swati Srivastava and Avnesh Kumar deal with lesbian relationship and feminist awakening in *A Married Woman.* R. Jagatheeswari's study is on the emergence of New Woman in *A Married Woman.*

Alice Rossi makes feministic analysis of discrimination against women and deconstructs the traditional patriarchal constructs to pick up their voices against repression and sex-subjugation. Talluri Mathew Bhaskar covers the issues of identity, inequality factors, gender discrimination and exploitation as the second sex. Farzan S. Ali, K.K. Singh and Chandra Bhushan make critical study on women's perspective in novels of Manju Kapur.

Smriti Nagpal analyzes the quest of middle-class woman to survive, the need to create an identity for herself in patriarchal society. Sujatha Bamane studies the feminist dimensions in Jai Nimbkar's *Come Rain*. K. Balachandran makes a critical study of Jai Nimbkar's *Temporary Answers*. T.S. Borate studies love and marriage versus individual freedom in *Temporary Answers*. Joan Contracter and Rina Sarkar review *Temporary Answers* as an understanding of human nature. Vilas Salunke discusses the predicament of marriage as presented in *A Joint Venture*. T.S. Borate examines *A Joint Venture* from feminine-feminist-female consciousness.

The survey of criticism reveals that there has not been any study of Manju Kapur and Jai Nimbkar from the perspective of the emancipation of women. The present study attempts to fill this gap. It seeks to examine Manju Kapur's *Difficult Daughters* and *A Married Woman* and Jai Nimbkar's *Joint Venture* and *Temporary Answers* with a focus on their portrayal of the emancipation of woman in the changing context of modern times from a comparative perspective.

The study is divided into six chapters. The first chapter discusses the development of Indian English fiction written by women writers. The second chapter focuses on struggle for feminist autonomy and identity in *Difficult Daughters*. It is the story of a girl finding her inner self. Virmati rebels against the family, pursues her studies and gets recognition as a principal. But the illicit affair with Harish, an America-returned professor, stalls her progress. Though Harish marries her after all the ups and downs, she finds herself on the crossroads. Differences arise in the family because Harish is a married man with children. Virmati stays as a second wife. Her experiences at her husband's place give her strength and confidence to take her own decisions and not run away from life; she faces the situations boldly. The novel ends with the pathetic death of Virmati, even the wish to bury her as she wanted is not fulfilled. Education gets her respect in society but the illicit affair cripples her individuality.

The third chapter examines quest for autonomy and empowerment in *A Married Woman.* Astha, the protagonist, is a rebel who as a teenager has affairs with Rohan and Bunty. She exchanges the orthodox family for the conventions of the "smart young set" of the city. Later she marries America-returned Hemant. Hemant frequently goes abroad for business. Astha is depressed about her married life and tries to be a good wife. She enjoys the marital bliss for some time but later develops a lesbian relationship with Pipee, wife of her friend Aijaz. She neglects family and children in search of peace but realizes that she is building castles in the air by staying with Pipee and that their relationship has no value. Her emancipation, which she thinks she got through the job, friendship with Aijaz and lesbian relationship, becomes illusory. At the end of the novel, she leaves Pipee and goes back to Hemant who learns to attend to her needs.

The fourth chapter discusses idiosyncrasy of patriarchy and reconciliation in *A Joint Venture*. Jyoti, the protagonist of the novel, decides to leave her husband after thirty years of marriage. She is from a middle-class family and works as a bank employee till she meets Ram. Ram is from a rich family; he proposes to Jyoti as she is different from other girls. He does not demand dowry and wants a simple marriage. After marriage, Jyoti moves to Ram's village though she is brought up in the city. She moulds herself according to their in-laws and takes the responsibilities of farming: employs workers and helps them in their need. She feels an emancipated woman organizing the things. She enjoys the work and is completely involved in it. After a period of time, Ram starts Triveni Seeds business and makes Jyoti his partner. As the business grows, their marriage is on the rocks. She is unhappy when he takes all the decisions: having a party at home, naming ceremony of children, or sending the children to boarding school. His fraudulent steps in business make Jyoti leave him. Ram plans a trip to Mahabaleshwar to make her change her mind. However, Jyoti leaves him. Later through Vinnie, Jyoti learns that Ram has been cheated by his rival in business and Ram is close to bankruptcy. Learning about the incident, Jyoti comes back to help Ram. Ram regrets what had happened. The novel reveals that Jyoti makes her husband establish the business again.

The penultimate chapter discusses difficulties of widowhood in *Temporary Answers*. Vineeta, the protagonist of the novel, is widowed in her thirties. She is a doctor by profession but does not practise after getting married to Nagendra. Nagendra does not demand any dowry which impresses her. She enjoys the bliss of married life for some time, but is tired of Nagendra's attitude as he spends much of the time with his cronies. Vineeta wishes to be with Nagendra but he spends much of his time outdoors, which bothers her. After the death of Nagendra, she comes in contact with Vilas, her childhood friend, who comes to India for good. He is also a doctor by profession. He helps Vineeta to start her practice and also wants to marry her. Vineeta does not want to marry Vilas because he considers her weak and fragile. She later develops sexual relationship with Abhijit Gokhale and thinks he may be the right person to marry as both have similar thinking. However, she feels that all men are alike and not considerate to women. Their relationship ends with separation. Vineeta realizes that marriage is a temporary answer and the relationship with Vilas, Nagendra and Abhijit were temporary answers.

The concluding chapter gives a comparative overview of the four novels *Difficult Daughters, A Married Woman, Joint Venture* and *Temporary Answers.* The study, it is hoped, will offer useful insights into the rapidly changing tendency of educated career women towards institutions of family and marriage.

Struggle for Feminist Autonomy and Identity in Manju Kapur's *Difficult Daughters*

Manju Kapur is a novelist of international repute. Born in Amritsar, she did M.A. in English from Dalhousie University in Halifax, Canada, and M.Phil. from Delhi University. She taught at Miranda College, New Delhi, for over three decades and took voluntary retirement to become a full-time writer. Her first novel *Difficult Daughters*, published in 1998, received huge international acclaim and was awarded the Commonwealth Writers Prize for the best first book.

Her novels *A Married Woman* (2003) and *Home* (2006) were shortlisted for the Hutch Crossword Prize for fiction, *The Immigrant* (2008) was shortlisted for the DSC Prize. She also edited *Shaping the World: Women Writers on Themselves*, a work that documents the literary journey of twenty-four women writers.

The novel *Difficult Daughters* presents conflict between tradition and modernity. It documents accurately the life and time of the nation's early years. The year 1947 not only brought independence from the British Empire and the painful holocaust of partition, it also brought separation from the past values and traditions. The background of the Second World War, colonialism and partition have recognized the potential of women who joined their male counterparts in societal rejuvenation and war against the rigid social code imposed upon them.

Kapur presents the defiant women breaking the conventional codes in the male-dominated society. Dora Sales Salvador, in notes to her Spanish Translation of this novel, points out: "Kapur emphasizes the efforts made at that time by numerous women who, while demanding equal opportunities, equal access to education and life opportunities going beyond convention, were a visible force in the non-violent resistance to the British." (361)

The story is of a middle-class home, with fathers, mothers, brothers and sisters. Manju Kapur shows that the institution of marriage has lost its sanctity and relevance in the present context. Lack of faith in traditional customs and decline of moral values are the main themes in her novels.

Virmati, the protagonist of the novel, was born in Amritsar in a conservative family. She is portrayed as an emancipated woman of colonial India challenging the reigning attitude of the society towards women. Commenting on it, Bhagabat Nayak remarks: "Manju Kapur seems to give tribute to the country's celebration of fifty years of independence in her novel as her protagonist Virmati is projected as a cult to impugn the set norms and taboos imposed on women in the male-dominated Indian society." (98)

The novel is set against the backdrop of the turbulent years of Indian freedom movement and the partition of India. Manju Kapur has intertwined the political upheaval of the 1950s with the changing feminist perspective of modern times.

The story unfolds women of three generations—Virmati, Ida and Kasturi and their sense of disillusionment. Kasturi, mother of Virmati and the grandmother of Ida, represents the pre-independence period. Ida and Virmati are products of the post-independence era. Virmati symbolizes the country's struggle for independence on a macro level as the time duration is from the nineteen thirties to the present. Virmati creates lines of partition in her parental family as well as in the family of her husband.

The times of freedom struggle have traditional women of the first generation: Kasturi, Lajwanti, Harish's mother, Kishori Devi and his first wife, Ganga. They give priority to the family and think that "it is the duty of every girl to get married." (15) Ganga's view of marriage is that "some things come before studies." (41) Ganga, the wife of Harish Chandra, glorifies the institution of marriage and strongly believes that marriage is the ultimate aim of a girl's life.

The second generation Virmati, Shakuntala and Swarnalata rebel against the age-old traditions. Shakuntala's thinks "beyond a husband and children" and does not marry. She tells Virmati that all her "friends are from different backgrounds, and all have families unhappy with their decision not to settle down." (17) They are emancipated women. The third generation includes Virmati's daughter Ida, and the Professor's daughter, Chotti who joins IAS and does not marry as she has been a witness to the disastrous marriage of her parents. Virmati and Ida are plagued with the limits of the system which cannot perceive change. Ida goes through a painful marriage and an equally painful divorce and strives for space within the patriarchal society, a 'room' of her own in a male-dominated society.

Virmati's mother Kasturi does not allow her the freedom to pursue her studies when she fails in F.A. She falls in love with a married man and marries him to be his second wife, which is considered illicit and does not receive any social, legal sanction. She goes through abortion, which results in her being marginalized by her own family and husband. Virmati, in search of emancipation and better things in life, takes the road less travelled and begins to get education.

Virmati rebels against deep-rooted conventions set by society for a girl. She realizes that there is life beyond the horizons which are still to unfold. Annie John writes: "Although Virmati succeeds in breaking all man-made boundaries, there are certain priorities so deeply embedded within her that she struggles to shake through the shackles. She grows up from a naïve girl to a woman matured by suffering and through experience."

Manju Kapur delves deep into a woman's inner turmoil and encourages her to seek an identity. Ashok Kumar writes: "In a culture where individualism and protest have often remained alien ideas and marital bliss and the women's role at home are in focus, it is interesting to see the emergence of not just an essential Indian sensibility but an expression of cultural displacement. Manju Kapur has joined the growing number of women writers from India on whom the image of the suffering, but the stoic woman eventually breaking traditional boundaries has had a significant impact" (48).

The novel *Difficult Daughters* focuses on the issues of gender discrimination, the struggle for emancipation of the distressed women under the unfair mechanism of patriarchal society. It is the tale of a bold woman who has courage and strength to fight her own battle for emancipation.

Difficult Daughters begins with Ida's narration about her late mother Virmati. She is the product of the post-independence era who braves herself as an independent woman. Ida, who has gone through her divorce, starts the quest in a bid to find her individuality. She recalls her mother's last words: "there should be no shor shaar and her eyes, heart, kidneys and other useful organs should be donated." (1)

Ida observes all the rituals in a manner that conflicted with her mother's wish and starts her journey to visit her birthplace to find an insight into her mother's past. She boards a train to visit her mother's place, without informing anyone about her arrival and moves to different places, meeting her mother's relatives and acquaintances to know every aspect of her mother's life from her relatives. Ida's anguish about her mother echoes in her opening words. "The one thing I wanted was not to be like my mother. Now she was gone and I started at the fire that rose from her shrivelled body, dry-eyed, leaden, half dead myself, while my relatives clustered around the pyre and wept." (1)

Ida gathers information about Virmati's life who as the eldest daughter of eleven children of Kasturi and Suraj Prakash, spends her time as the second mother, overburdened with household work. She learns that her mother's siblings look up to her for every little thing as Kasturi is often pregnant, leaving the young ones to be looked after by Virmati. Virmati accepts the domestic responsibilities, but at times feels "trapped in the house and moaned about ruthlessly." (11) Virmati's childhood is dampened with the responsibilities of an eldest daughter. She yearns for affection from her mother but fails to get it.

> When she puts her head next to the youngest baby, feeding in the mother's arms, Kasturi would get irritated and push her away. 'Have you seen to their food—milk—clothes—studies?' . . . 'I am just going,' protests Virmati finally. 'Why can't Indumati also take responsibility? Why does it always have to be me?' 'You know they don't listen to her,' snapped Kasturi. 'You are the eldest. If you don't see things, who will? (6-7)

She is constantly reminded that she is the eldest and it is her duty to look after her siblings. Virmati has no sweet memories of childhood; she remembers only looking after her siblings. The one cause for Virmati's frustration was her mother's continuous breeding. It wasn't only baby Parvati to whom she was indispensable; to her younger siblings, she was the second mother. (6)

Virmati mutely watches her weak, ailing mother go through long years of childbearing. Kasturi's notion is "Woman's Shaan is in her home" (13)--to give birth to children and take care of their upbringing, all the time fulfilling the needs of her husband and other men in the family. She is brought up in a patriarchal society where marriage is the ultimate destiny of a girl's life: "She is a traditional woman and is confined to childbearing and kitchen work. She felt grateful to her mother for those long hours she has spent in the kitchen, cutting, peeling, chopping, slicing, pounding, wrapping, mixing, kneading, baking, roasting, stirring and frying." (188-89)

Kasturi feels that she will please her in-laws by doing the household work and also feels that her education means developing the mind for the benefit of the family and nothing more than that. She is the first girl in her family to postpone the wedlock for a tentative learning. She learned to read, sew, write and balance household accounts. The rituals of Arya Samaj such as Havan, Sandhya and meditation are deep rooted in her. After five years of rigorous and disciplined education, she appears for her first and last exam. At the age of twelve, her education is over and she stays at home until she's married. Kasturi's education testifies Millett's remarks in *Sexual Politics*: "The education of women was not thought of as a course of study beyond the threshold level of learning, a genteel polish and its major achievement. And in most cases, it was deliberately cynical in its emphasis upon virtue, a sugared word which meant obedience, servility, and a sexual inhibition perilously near to frigidity" (74).

The structure of education was such that it emphasized the balance between education and household responsibilities. "Kasturi's formal education was never forgotten that marriage was her destiny. After her graduation, her education continued in the home." (62) Arya Samaj did bring about a few important ideological changes and transformed a traditional society into a modern one. For instance, it discouraged child marriage and encouraged women's education.

Kasturi tries to implement the same on Virmati who rejects domesticity, marriage, and childbearing--all that her mother stands for, "it hardly made a difference to the real business of hers, which was getting married and looking after her own home." (19) She never feels one with her mother and says: "I will live my life." (66)

Virmati's quest for identity, her desperation in finding space for study and her desire to shed the surrogate motherhood imposed on her makes her traumatic. Virmati longs for Virmati longs for--love and understanding but Kasturi doesn't have time for her. "The language of feeling had never flowed between them." (12) Virmati started her schooling at the Arya Kanya Mahavidyalaya: "Virmati finishes her class VIII and has been sent for higher studies to Stanford College in the Civil Lines, after that, class IX and X, and then two years to get a Fine Arts degree. And then marriage said the elders. . . . Thirteen-year-old Virmati listened and felt the thrill of those approaching rites." (17)

Virmati desires to study but has to look after the household. All the time, there are demanding noises. Eventually, Virmati fails her FA (Fine Arts). Her mother says that it is over now and creates a great fuss. Virmati is frustrated at her failure. On this, Kasturi says: "Leave your studies if it is going to make you so bad tempered with your family. You are forgetting what comes first." (21) Virmati tries to come out of the frustration of her failure in studies and looks up to Shakuntala, her cousin, who sows seeds of freedom in Virmati: "These people don't really understand Viru. Women are still supposed to marry and nothing else." (17) As her mother intervenes in her wish to a new world of knowledge and self-assurance, a world to which her mother has no access, she resents. Betty Friedan's *The Feminine Mystique* questions why a woman in a patriarchal system is confined to domesticity and childcare: "For the woman, as for man, the need for self-fulfillment—the autonomy, self-realization, independence, individuality, and self-actualization—is as important as the sexual need." (282)

Lajwanti and Kasturi disagree with the ideas of Shakuntala; they believe that man is free to do his desire and woman has to take every step according to the norms of society. They admonish Shakuntala for supporting Virmati's desire to continue her studies. Shakuntala has an attitude of emancipation for women which Virmati is attracted to. Kasturi is against Shakuntala's thought and says: "All the time in the lab, doing experiments, helping the girls, studying or going to conferences, I tell her she should have been a man" (16). Shakuntala did not stop influencing Virmati. Simone de Beauvoir says that the two prerequisites for women's freedom are "economic independence and liberation from orthodox traditions of society." (126)

As the conversation about Virmati's further education takes place between Shakuntala and her mother, her mother once again falls sick. The doctor advises Kasturi to take rest to overcome her ailment. Her father-in-law decides to send Kasthuri to a nearby hill station for recuperation. Virmati has to accompany her ailing mother to the hill station on doctor's advice. Lajwanti, the wife of Virmati's elder uncle, is envious about Kasturi leaving for hill station and tries to incite her husband to stop her: "How irresponsible to expect to be pampered like this. . . . Really, some women have no sense." (11) She further says that Kasturi "is no better than a dog or cat in season." (22) Instead of sympathizing with her sister-in-law and trying to help her, she disagrees with her father-in-law, who says Kasturi's children bring "raunaq in the house." (22)

Lajwanti complains to her husband Chander Prakash about the growing noise of the children and the money spent on them. Her father-in-law is going to retire soon and she wants division in the family but Lala Diwan Chand is against it; he doesn't want the family to be divided until his death: "As long as he was alive, everybody would be provided for. But with each new child Kasturi produced, the murmurs of discontent became louder and more persistent." (25)

The problems start cropping up when his father says if the money or property is divided, everything will be divided equally. Lajwanti retorts: "Baoji, they are eleven, and we are two. How will everything be equal?" (26). Lala Diwan Chand wishes to move to Lepel Griffin Road especially for ailing Kasturi to stop the conflicts at home. Lajwanti offers to go to Dalhousie to help Kasturi at hill station: "Ostensibly to assist Kasturi, after all, there was only Virmati there to look after her and her, a mere child! . . . She must stay as long as possible, to assist the invalid on her road to recovery. She herself also needed some rest occasionally." (12)

Shifting to Lepel Griffin Road from Amritsar is a blessing in disguise to Virmati as Shakuntala visits the place often and plants "the seeds of aspiration in Virmati." (17) Shakuntala inspires her to study further. She has the same background but is intelligent enough to shape her life. She resists the family's pressure about her marriage by making her priorities clear in life.

Shakuntala has done her M.Sc. in Chemistry and has tasted "the wine of freedom" (18) which gives her power to get free from the shackles of patriarchy. Virmati wants to follow her advice:

> 'Maybe I will also one day come to Lahore, Pehnji,' she wept. 'I wish I too could do things, But I am not clever'—'Arre,' exclaimed her cousin patting her on the back, 'times are changing and women are moving out of the house, so why not you?' Why not, indeed, thought Virmati looking at her, almost breathless with admiration and love. (18)

Virmati decided to go to Lahore, even if "she had to fight her mother to make sure that her education is not practically over." (17) Kasturi tells Virmati that there are other important things in a girl's life--getting married, having children, setting up a home and having domestic bliss. The defiant and assertive Virmati, symbolizing the country's struggle for independence, has a craving for emancipation and psychologically reveals her rebellious nature by challenging deep-rooted conventions of morality.

Virmati wants to go away from her mother and finds education to be an escape from the reproaches of her family and control by her mother. Virmati looks up to Shakuntala for help; they are called difficult daughters of the family as they represent the evolving consciousness of the modern Indian woman. Shakuntala rejects marriage and studies further. Kasturi resents Shakuntala's lifestyle of rejecting marriage and staying away from home for the sake of a job. Shakuntala challenges the established norms with her liberated views on marriage and education. Kate Millett's observes in *Sexual Politics*: "While modern patriarchies have, fairly recently, opened all educational levels to women, the kind and quality of education are not the same for each sex. This difference is, of course, apparent in early socialization, but it persists and enters into higher education as well." (42)

Shakuntala influences Virmati to break the customs of the tradition-bound society and to realize that the clue to her happiness lies outside the house. Virmati is impressed by the activities of her cousin: "She watches her ride horses, smoke, play cards and badminton, act without her mother's advice, and buy anything she wanted, and above all, she never seemed to question or doubt herself in anything." (15) She pesters her family to send her to Lahore for further studies and finally they agree. Virmati moves to college and shows interest in "education, freedom, and the bright lights of Lahore colleges." (17) She breaks the manacles with the determination to reach the goal. She grows up from an adolescent girl to a woman mature enough to experience the suffering at home. All plans are set for Virmati to join the college. The parents seek advice from Harish Chandra, an English Professor, who is a tenant of Lajwanti (Virmati's paternal aunt) on Lepel Griffin Road. Virmati's mother feels confident about Virmati's future after studying at the college.

Harish Chandra's wife Ganga is also quite supportive in guiding them. Harish tries to get his wife educated but fails as she shows interest not in studies but in cooking and feeding her family. She was married at the age of twelve and is proficient in embroidery, knitting needles and the sewing machine. After her marriage, she learns the ways of her in-laws' household. De Beauvoir comments on women's education and economy: "The truth is that her situation is out of equilibrium. Women are still, for the most part, in a state of subjection. It follows that woman sees herself and makes her choices not in accordance with her true nature in itself, but as man defines her." (167-69)

A close relationship develops between the families of Harsh Chandra and Virmati. The Oxford-returned Professor Harish Chandra notices Virmati as she sits in the front row in the class along with four other girls and four hundred boys: "Flower-like, against the backdrop of male students." (42) The Professor "drank in the symbolism of her posture greedily. It moved him so deeply that he remembered it in all its detail . . . the Professor's desire to possess had extended to her heart and mind." (46-47)

Since Vedic era, female body has been seen as an object by man. V. Geeta writes about social attitude: "Women's bodies were often routinely viewed as objects of male desire and lust; a fact that was particularly evident in media images of women. Women's groups pointed to the range of sexual crimes that were directed at women—child abuse, incest, marital rape—to argue that their social existence was invariably sexualized and therefore not seen as worthy of equality or justice. The family and larger kin group, they noted, actively aided this sexualization of women's bodies by valorizing against women, they insisted, which secured the patriarch's power, both at level of family and society." (191)

Harish Chandra begins to lend books to Virmati, forces her to stay for tea and gives her admiring looks. He is attracted by the look of her face. On the other hand, Virmati considers this to be his concern for her education. For the first time, something interests her outside home: "He was offering a little bit of himself, which both flattered and alarmed Virmati." (39) Virmati did not know the world outside; the attention of the professor makes her feel the world of romance. Harish Chandra did not think he would ever fall in love with his student Virmati who was passionate for studies. Though married, Harish Chandra craves for her attention and shares his feelings with Virmati: "What it takes me away from the women I live with? Apart from the planets in the house of marriage, of course! She is a good woman, runs the house to perfection, and looks after my family as though they were her own. Despite all this, I am lonely, lonely, and lonely." (103)

For Harish Chandra, Virmati is pliant clay to be moulded into the creature he has in mind. "He loves to teach her and instructs her to shape her perceptions of the world around her. He looked at her with the eyes of a Pygmalion." (115) Virmati is attracted towards the sophisticated life of the professor who is well-versed in English literature especially poetry. His gestures make Virmati realize: "It was useless looking for answers inside the home. One had to look outside. To educate, freedom and the bright lights of Lahore colleges." (17)

At home, the talk about Virmati's marriage starts but she persuades her family not to go ahead with this. Kasturi finds this unreasonable and yells: "At your age, I was already expecting you, not fighting with my mother" (19). She knows that her parents expect from her "nothing . . . but an agreement to marry." (100)

At the age of 17, her mother finds a match for her in Inderjeet, a canal engineer. Virmati's in-laws think that she is qualified enough to be their daughter-in-law and there is no need to study further; but Virmati refuses the marriage proposal. Her mother slaps her, shouts at her and locks her up in the godown for refusing the marriage proposal. Unable to take the insult and shouts of her mother, Virmati decides to commit suicide. She walks up to Tarsikka in the late afternoon. The servant of their family saves her and brings her back to Lepel Griffin Road. Her parents do not know her inner feelings and mental turmoil. However, they declare that she does not like the boy and wants to study further. The bridegroom chosen for Virmati is settled to Indumati the second daughter. Commenting on her defiance of patriarchal society, Dipika Sahai opines: "The hardship and suffering involved in fighting against an established order, the shattering experience of rejection by her family on becoming the second wife of the professor, and the resultant alienation from society forms the theme of the novel. Her life is a continuous struggle. She wants to establish an order through defiance. She rebels against the accepted and existing moral codes and social norms." (8)

Virmati believes that Professor and she are bound together by intellectual compatibility and reacts adversely to Harish's irresolute attitude. Harish's physical lust overpowers him whenever they are together. Virmati's desire to be like her cousin Shakuntala is unfulfilled and the education she gets is useless. Commenting on her illicit relationship, S. Prasanna Sree says: "Virmati struggles between the physical and moral, the head and heart. Finally, she gives way to her heart and body. Virmati is engaged to an engineer initially but series of incidents propel the family members to postpone the wedding. This incident paves way for Virmati to begin an illicit relationship with the married Professor living next door. Virmati undergoes the trials and tribulations of love that has little hope of social acceptance. The Oxford-returned Professor finds little to share with his uneducated wife and is unable to resist the charms of Virmati, who is innocent and hungry for knowledge and love." (175)

Virmati and Harish maintain distance but continue their relationship through letters, now and then she meets Professor at his home. Harish wants to have Virmati not as his wife but as a woman to gratify his physical needs. In the words of Dr. Maji: "The book starts with the problems that married couples encounter and experience when there is no love lost between them. Kapur reveals without taking anybody's side the power of the extra-marital affair which can break up even a solid marriage. Morals and ethics don't work and have no place when it comes to love." (2)

Virmati is disturbed by the illicit affair and the step she has taken. Although she tells the world that she is going to Lahore for further studies, in reality, it is an attempt to find respite from the professor. Virmati wants to explore life beyond the ordinary life like her cousin Shakuntala. Both Shakuntala and Virmati come out of the grotto of being a typical Indian woman. Shakuntala actively moves around in the political field influenced by Gandhian movement, Virmati also follows her cousin.

Virmati and her friend Swarnalatha converse about the consequences of the communal tension at the time of Indian freedom struggle. Gurpyari Jandial comments: "With Swarnalatha, Virmati attends Punjab Women's Student Conference. She hears women who exude confidence and strength. She listens to them as they explain the meaning of the flag, the importance of freedom for the development of human spirit, impact of war, human rights, strikes, academic freedom, rural upliftment, language etc." (96)

Virmati feels isolated by sitting there, listening to Mohini Datta's speech on how freedom was necessary for the development of human spirit, how the war affected women, how progress is their object so that freedom is enjoyed by everyone. Her hostel roommate Swarnalata tries to shake her up from her "stale dream" (139) and divert her to other objectives in life that could help her stay out of the Professor's way.

She tells Harish not to visit her until her BT exam over. But she does not stick to her word and meets him secretly. Away from familial vigilance, she is distracted by the Professor, who meets Virmati regularly. He stays at his friend Syed's guest house in Lahore to fulfill his physical desire. She yields to the professor's passion and this leads to her pregnancy before BT exams. The independence she enjoyed finally dooms her. She tries to send the message to Harish about her pregnancy, not knowing how to face the situation. She wants to take Harish's advice but the message does not reach him. As the exams are approaching, she remains mentally disturbed and gets the child aborted with the help of Swarnalata. Virmati does not fare well in her exams due to her relationship with Harish. Swarna tries to console her: "Swarna's words gave her some comfort. But that meant thinking of a life for herself without marriage, which was strange and not quite right. It meant she would be alone, and she wasn't sure she was capable of it." (140)

Knowing that the professor will not render any support to her in such hours of crisis, Virmati decides to save her family from shame. After completing her exams, she leaves for Lahore only. She learns about Harish's wife's pregnancy and the inner conflict makes Virmati isolate herself. Her confusion grows as days pass: "She would sometimes wish that . . . what could she wish? Early marriage and no education? No Professor and no love? Her soul revolted and her sufferings increased." (54)

Harish had filled her emptiness with love but that was also the cause of the obstacles in her life. Harish lacks courage to accept Virmati as wife. Though he could not love his illiterate wife, yet he could not leave her. Virmati questions herself: "Am I free . . .? I came here to be free, but I am not like these women. They are using their minds, organizing, participating in conferences, politically active, while my time is spent being in love. Wasting it. Well, not wasting time, no, of course not, but then how come I never have a moment for anything else? Swarna does." (142)

Virmati feels that she is in chains as she underwent the abortion due to the pressure of the social norms. Manju Kapur deals with the theme of travails in self-identity vis-à-vis socio-cultural identity. In this context, Toni Morrison remarks: "Tell us what it is to be a woman so that we may know what it is to be a man. What moves at the margin? What it is to have no home in this place. To be set adrift from the one you knew. What it is to live at the edge of towns that cannot bear your company." (201)

Virmati feels the pain of womanhood; she had come to Lahore to increase her mental horizons but has ended up in useless and meaningless love relationship. Malik opines: "She wanted to do 'something meaningful' in her life like her roommate Swarnalata, who was a freedom movement activist, but she failed to transcend her underlying need for love and emotional dependence." (135)

Virmati finds herself locked in new prisons even as she breaks old ones. She silently endures her pain and frustration, she fails to get out of her emotional craving for the professor, but she is moved by Swarnalata's words, that marriage is not the only thing in life. Virmati tries to realizes the real meaning of being a woman.

When Ida learns from her relatives about her mother's abortion and suffering, she is reminded of her own abortion on her husband Prabhakar's insistence. The comparison makes her feel that she is more mature and strong-willed than her mother. Though she has endured the harrowing experience of abortion, she never forgave her husband Prabhakar for depriving her the bliss of motherhood. The idea to defy her husband did not come to her mind and the lack of virtue in him makes her walk out of the relationship. She does not want to maintain a relationship that is fake and hollow like that of her mother Virmati.

Ida is far from the traditional women who suffered believing, 'It is all my Karma.' (173) Virmati enters a new phase in life when she gets an opportunity to work at Nahan. With her BA and BT degree, Virmati is selected as a suitable candidate to fill the vacant post in the school. Her parents object to her taking up a job: "We did not educate her to send her away to work. She is still so simple and inexperienced." (165) Diwan persuades her family members to agree to his offer and leaves.

Kasturi is not willing to send Virmati for job but Suraj Prakash cajoles Virmati and tells her if she is not going to marry, she can do something else instead of sitting idle at home; he encourages her to take up the job. The topic of marriage comes up again, only to make Virmati violent. After the Tarsikka episode, the family is too wary to force her to do anything against her will. They let Virmati accept the job: "Girl's education is seen as a way of adapting to the changing times. It is also perceived as an unfortunate necessity for, as the Diwan Sahib of Nahan, where Virmati takes up her first job, puts it; it encourages girls to be independent and wayward." (181)

Virmati goes to Nahan, the capital of Sirmaur, the small Himalayan state run by an enlightened Maharaja. She enjoys working as the headmistress at a girl's school. She finally achieves control over her life at Nahan. Her performance wins her respect and honour at school. Virmati gets a fresh start at Nahan and waits to taste the wine of emancipation as she did in Lahore.

Virmati concentrates on her career. Proud to be the headmistress of Pratibha Kanya Vidyalaya, she takes care of her home. The days pass happily with a busy schedule. A single or widowed lady teacher or headmistress is something of a stock figure in modern Indian literature. Virmati attains a near-exemplary level of female autonomy. For the first and only time, she has her own place to live. She is at last an emancipated woman with full confidence and strength. Susan Polis Schultz says: "The new woman arises full of confidence, she speaks eloquently and thinks independently, full of strength. She organizes efficiently and directs proudly." (39).

Virmati handles the school which has two hundred and fifty girls who come from the homes of traders, shopkeepers, bankers, teachers and the state employees of Samar. Virmati has grown up shouldering responsibilities at home and has enough talent to handle things. She supervises the accounts, gives appointments to parents, holds weekly meetings with the teachers, monthly meetings with the prime minister, and the occasional meetings with the Maharani Pratibha. In the evenings, when she is briskly sauntering around the hillside, she recollects what she has done in the day and feels satisfied.

However, many a time she longs for the Professor. Virmati is yet to realize that for her "love and autonomy could never co-exist." (169) The situation inside and outside the home agonizes her. She tries to keep distance from her family and the prying eyes of the strangers on the road.

She seeks a fresh start not for herself but for her relationship with the Professor also. The loneliness makes her communicate with the Professor again. This shows how weak and fluctuating she is in taking decisions. She writes to Harish that she perceives her stay at Nahan as a period of waiting rather than the beginning of a career. In a way, she also threatens Harish to make up his mind to marry her or she will devote herself to her career.

Harish gets the information about Virmati's workplace and repeats his secret visits. Her description of life at Nahan where she works as a principal fires Harish's romantic imaginations and he begins to meet her. She vacillates between her career and her marriage to Harish. Frequent visits by the professor make her employers lose confidence in her and she has to quit her job.

When Harish meets her, Virmati lets the devils raging inside her come out in the open. For the first time, she gives vent to her seething anger. She scolds Harish when he shows his helplessness to marry her: "I break my engagement because of you, blacken my family's name, being locked up inside my house, get sent to Lahore because no one knows what to do with me. Here I am in the position of being your secret wife, full of shame, wondering what people will say if they find out, not being able to live in peace, study in peace . . . and why? Because I am an idiot. I can bear anything but this continuous irresolution. Swarna is right Men do take advantage of women!" (137-38)

"Virmati has achieved through Harish, education, work, marriage and suffering." (253) The lesson is "adjust, compromise, adapt" (256) to place. Virmati tramples over the "outmoded morality." (114) Nonetheless, years of conditioning leave its benchmark on her psyche; she pesters Harish to marry her and make things clear to everybody. Virmati never realizes that both of them are cowards to face the world. Manju Verma aptly points out: "The relationship between the two could have been an ideal between a man and a woman but unfortunately it becomes a story of an exploiter and an exploited, a union of un-equals, and an unusual tale of male chauvinism and woman's total submission." (171)

Harish is not sure whether his marriage with Virmati would be acceptable to his family. He makes the best use of both the worlds. He needs Ganga, his legal wife, to dish him his favourite eateries at home and maintain his "starched dhoti-kurta" image; he needs Virmati for sexual satisfaction. No matter how bravely Harish claims that co-wives are a part of the society, inwardly he is afraid of his family.

In spite of knowing the reality, Virmati lacks the courage to tear herself away from the Professor. Every time her emotions betray her and she falls prey to the Professor's cunningness. Arpita Ghosh remarks: "Virmati fell prey to Professor Harish's desire. Slowly but surely such desire swallowed up Virmati; she transgressed the laws of the threshold and got involved in an illicit affair with Harish both physically and mentally. He forcefully enters the cottage and makes love without Virmati's prior consent to the act. In spite of Virmati's protest, Harish beastly pounces on her and quenches his thirst for lust. Thus another violence committed in liaison, Virmati was doomed forever." (126)

The Professor represents the patriarchal authority and has always relegated woman's needs to obscurity. Virmati's outburst out makes him feel humiliated beyond imagination. He was unable to bear such "insensitivity" on Virmati's part and leaves the place immediately.

Virmati is sacked from the job; the school authorities ask her to leave the place as soon as the year comes to an end. Her position and emancipation have once again brought disgrace to her family. This time she doesn't have the courage to face her family and starts her journey eastwards to Shanti Niketan.

Virmati's life is a graph of ups and downs in her life, which indirectly makes her strong to develop the will power to face the world. "She feels out of place, an outcast amongst all the women. She thought of Harish who loved her. She must be satisfied with that. These larger spaces were not for her. She felt an impostor sitting in the hall. Again, scenes from her private life came unbidden before her eyes." (144)

Virmati lacks 'resistance.' She does resist her family and society but fails to resist Harish's love. She is compelled to lead a life of compromise and finds no escape. Commenting on the dichotomy in Virmati, P. Sudha Sree aptly says: "There is an unresolved dichotomy in the character portrayal of Virmati, the female protagonist. While she is strong-willed to resist all kinds of social pressures, she is not strong enough to stay away from Professor's influence." (175) Her relationship with Harish makes her suffer pangs of guilt: "As for me, I know I have failed in my duty and I will be punished one day. Nobody can escape their *karma*. Maybe what is happening to me now is part of it, and there is no use protesting." (85)

She has always been a weak player in terms of emotion and Harish easily traps her with emotional blackmails. Harish studies Virmati's psychological as well as physical environment, skillfully. She is never been touched by any male outside the family and that too with molesting urge. She is neither able to enjoy with family nor with Harish. She couldn't think of any celebration with Harish especially the Diwali celebration which she visualizes as "a step towards public statement, matrimony and the fruition of love." (115) It is easy for Virmati to resist the patriarchs and deceive the matriarchs in her family, but with a foreign-returned patriarch like Harish, she is left defenceless.

She accepts Harish's whimsicalities unquestioningly. She has to prove her trust to Harish and she succumbs to the demands without any thought. Months later, each of Harish's words echo in her mind with an ironical touch. Her studies are her passport to independence and not just the passport to sleep with him

Virmati lives away from home for almost a year, she has seen women growing in power and strength, claiming responsibility for their lives declaring that society would be better if female is effective and capable. She wants to solve her problems on her own. She is worthy of emancipation.

Virmati comes across a poet friend of Harish during these difficult circumstances. He takes liberty and requests Virmati to stay at his place, in the meantime he sends a telegram to Harish to reach Calcutta as soon as possible. Harish does rush to Calcutta but evades the question of marriage. Many a time she asks Harish to marry her but every time, he postpones it. With her exams round the corner, Virmati recalls her bitter row with the Professor in the past; she has read his eyes and the uncertainty in his voice. She does not have enough courage to go back to her family as she is sure that she has smeared her family's name. She plans to meet Harish on her return to Amritsar during study leave, but fails to get in contact with him and learns that Harish has gone to his village house with the entire family for his baby boy's "mundan." (2) Virmati questions Harish about not informing her in advance. He says: "My mother insisted the baby's mundan be done in the village, nobody there has seen him, you know and I thought it was a good opportunity to go since you had decided I should leave you alone. Now you are being unfair! I can't help it if something happened. I was so careful." (176)

Professor Harish lacks the will-power and courage of a man truly in love. Though educated abroad in English literature, which is quite liberating and strengthening at the same time, he dares not displease his family. Virmati takes the help of Harish's poet friend who asks him either to accept Virmati as a wife or let her go. "Be prepared to let her go." (185) This puts him in uncomfortable situation. "He dreaded facing his family." but he was "soothed with the achievement of his desires." (190) After a lot of persuasion from his friend, Harish finally takes the step of marrying Virmati. Harish is worried if his wife and children will accept it.

Virmati finally marries the man she loves and returns to Amritsar. Harish refuses to leave his first wife and Virmati has to stay as second wife and is not considered a member of the family. She stays as an outsider.

Ida learns from her relatives how her mother was appreciated for breaking the chains of tradition and leading an emancipated life. Ida learns about her mother's efforts to study: "Even after her marriage she studies M.A. at Government College, Lahore, she studied more than any other girl in their family and Harish Bhai Shahib—your father—was very particular about education. 'But why do you want all this? What is past is past, forget about it. Eat, have another paratha, you are so thin, my relatives gave me one view of my mother, I wanted another." (5)

Woman is confined to household chores on the pretext of virtuosity and security and treated as the 'other.' In this context, Simone De Beauvoir says: "The situation of woman is that she is a free and autonomous being like creatures—nevertheless finds herself living in a world where men compel her to assure the status of the other." (167)

Harish has snatched the rights of his first wife Ganga by marrying Virmati. Virmati has to suffer for it and has to live like an outsider in the family and also is marginalized by her in-laws. The burden of the life she spent without Harish lay heavy on Virmati's heart that seems to have lifted as she marries the Professor following the conventions and the rituals in the poet's house. Virmati's mother-in-law holds Virmati solely responsible for the marriage: "If she had not gone after him, he would not have strayed." (192) Harish's mother believes that he "was a good son. How was it his fault if he was caught in the trap of some shameless young Punjabi." (193) Virmati has to face her in-laws' grumbles because she has taken a wrong step. She repents and realizes that she has done wrong for which she faces discrimination in her in-laws' house. She also observes: "In the evening, Virmati goes to the angan to bring the clothes in. The line was bare except for her own, hanging for only at the end. She took them down and clenched her lips. She wondered drearily whether this isolation would continue until the end of her life." (215)

Harish is sometimes irritated with Virmati for making his life difficult by trying to share her rights with Ganga. Ganga's appearance doesn't change with her husband's second marriage. She continues to stay with them: "to be Ganga's public statement of selfhood. Her bindi and her bangles, her toe-rings and her mangal sutra, all managed to suggest that he was still her God." (278) He tries to console Virmati, saying: "You are my other self. Let her [Ganga] wash my clothes, if she feels like it. It has nothing to do with me. I don't want a washerwoman. I want a companion." (201)

Virmati suffers before marriage because she has an affair with a married man, after marriage Harish and his family impose restrictions on her. For the umpteenth time she uttered the same old words to the Professor:

> 'I should never have married you,' she said slowly, 'and it's too late now. I've never seen it so clearly. It's not fair.' She faltered and stopped. How many times in their past relationship has she said those very same words? I should not, cannot, will not marry you. It will not be fair. And now she had married him, but the old words were still springing to her lips, so many futile noises in the air. (212)

As the days pass, her "pariah status" is confirmed with every averted look. She was allowed to do nothing for Harish, except to share his bed at night. Being second wife of Harish, she loses all sense of identity. She has nothing else to do but concentrate on her studies and wait for Harish's return.

Virmati tries her best to mingle with the family and befriends Gudiya, her sister-in-law, who was not overtly hostile to her; she fails to win over Giridhar, Harish's son. Ganga gives a tight slap on her son's face who starts screaming "You want her to take him away too. One is not enough for that." (203) Virmati is disheartened when her father Suraj Prakash dies; she is blamed for his death because she married an already married man. Suraj Prakash feels sad about his daughter: "Baoji always looked pale and tired. After what his daughter did he was never the same. All last year so silent and listless. Everybody could notice. It killed him. Definitely killed him." (238) The next day, Virmati's grandfather Lala Diwan Chand also expires. Virmati feels a hardening around her heart listening to the news of the death and thinks nothing could remove her pain. She breaks down into tears and says that her father had died without forgiving her, and now her grandfather too had died. She feels wretched: "It was almost as though she had gone mad. Forgotten who she was, who she is married to and all her obligations." (240)

The loss of her father and grandfather gives more pain. All her life she suffered; only the short period at Nahan was the happy and successful phase of her life. As headmistress of the girls' school, she almost attained the autonomy over her life.

She fails to restrain herself from succumbing to the demands of the relationship which she knew from the beginning was doomed, but did not have the heart to deny. She hates to be the secret woman in Harish's life and wants to hide herself from prying eyes of the world. She was ostracized by her family and forced to compete with his first wife, Ganga, for her share of her husband's love. She was forced to compromise and adjust in order to adapt herself to her husband's family and eventually die an insignificant death. At the end of the novel, Ida says: "This book weaves a connection between my mother and me, each word-brick in a mansion I made with my head and my heart. Now live in it Mama and leave me be. Do not haunt me anymore." (108)

Virmati feels too tangled to focus on any one particular thing. Her relationship with the Professor leads her to so many new beginnings. The sense of hope was beginning to feel stale. Still, with every mile, she travels she feels stronger. There is a life of dedication and service ahead of her and in that she hopes to forge her identity. In all her ventures, she herself planted the seeds of disaster. Her attempt to meet Harish's poet friend hammered the final nail on her coffin and she was dumped back to the place from where she was fleeing for so long.

Ida wants to bury the ghosts of her mother's past and move on in life. At the end of the novel, Virmati's story gets swallowed in the greater tragedy of her death. Ida observes Virmati as a lonely woman who commits the unforgivable sin of carving an identity of her own. She is considered as a sinner to the backbone. When she dies, she is neither cremated according to her wishes nor is her voice recognized by anybody. Even her daughter Ida does not consider the ways of her mother justified. Ida says: "That was all she wanted to do. Forget, forget, forget, and forget. She felt a deep emptiness inside her, which she construed as a yearning for the Professor. Oh, how she longed to meet him, to throw herself on his chest, babble out her story, feel his love and sympathy, his regret that he wasn't there pouring over her in a great tidal wave that would cleanse her of all guilt and sorrow!" (173)

According to Ruby Malhotra, Virmati is the difficult daughter in the family of Lala Diwan Chand: "It is only Virmati who is the difficult daughter of the prosperous merchant family of Lala Diwan Chand. While in the generation of Kasturi, woman's role was confined to childbearing and kitchen work, the generation of Virmati took some bold and radical steps in joining the political movement for India's freedom, asserted the need for women's education and independence. As a nonchalant representative of the middle generation, Virmati breaks away from the tradition-bound limits of Indian women." (164)

Difficult Daughters is the story of a woman who struggles for freedom and emancipation in the initial years of modernization of India's economic and social conditions. The indecisiveness of Virmati throws her into many problems. While India combats for independence from the British Raj, Virmati struggles for the emancipation to live life on her terms. It is a wonderful saga of daughters who deal with hardships in their lives. Virmati is portrayed as a strong, emancipated and ambitious woman. and Harish as a caring, intelligent and understanding professor, life partner and a lover of his family who struggles between the love of his wife and a student. Their love story goes through many tests, facing equal assault from the chauvinists who declare woman's place is inside the house. It turns out as an earnest appeal for the sympathetic recognition of women's existence, and a redefinition of gender roles according to the changing socio-cultural contexts. The forceful expression is shown through the life and experience of different women characters. It is a forceful expression of Indian feminism and presents the most suitable feminist position for women's existence in traditional Indian society.

Kasturi seems to be quite helpless; her function is to produce children and look after the family. The only space available to her is inside the threshold, and 'shadi' she considers being the ultimate goal of a woman's life. For Kasturi, Shakuntala's life of singlehood is something unnatural and abnormal. Shakuntala moves around freely, attends conferences and likes to work in the laboratory. Kasturi comments, "I tell her she should have been a man." (14) Though 20th century brought much change in the Indian way of thinking, women like Kasturi dared not think of living without man's custody.

The reformist Arya Samaj movements and the Independence helps people to reject the traditions and give more opportunities to women. In *Difficult Daughters*, Manju Kapur portrays Indian women inclined towards westernization, which paved way for broader perspective in social and cultural life. Virmati craves for marriage with Harish despite all odds she encounters in her life. Though both the families disapprove their marriage, she goes ahead with it.

The novel deals with the idea of education and emancipation for a girl, not just to enable her to get a suitable match. Virmati carves her destiny through education; she gets a job and respect in society. She attains autonomy over her life and eventually discovered her own space to live. Like so many educated Indian girls, Virmati wants to decide on her own what to study and where, whom to marry and when. But she fails to restrain herself from succumbing to the demands of a relationship which was doomed from the beginning and ends up with compromise and adjustment in order to adapt herself to her husband's family and eventually dies an insignificant death.

Quest for Autonomy and Empowerment in Manju Kapur's *A Married Woman*

Manju Kapur is one of the postcolonial contemporary Indian English women writers who deal with the problems of women in a male-dominated Indian society. She emphasizes the changing image of women from traditional, meek, submissive to that of assertion, emancipation, quest for identity and individuality. Her literary work portrays the issues of male domination in Indian society. She sets her second novel *A Married Woman* in India of the late 1980s and early 1990s, balanced on the verge of globalization and explores two controversial subjects: Hindu-Muslim confrontation and intimacy of same-sex between women against a backdrop of respectable middle-class Delhi life. She uses the event of demolition of the Babri Masjid in Ayodhya by Hindu extremists as the backdrop. She documents *A Married Woman* with the themes of alienation, chauvinism and emancipation. The novel also deals with the lesbian extra-marital affairs of the protagonist.

Adrienne Rich in her essay 'Compulsory Heterosexuality and Lesbian Existence' published in 1980 challenges the naturalization of heterosexuality pointing out that heterosexuality is not 'natural' or innate, but in fact, it is an institution designed to perpetuate male social and economic privilege. She further opines that all relationships between women have some lesbian element, for example, mothers and daughters, women who work together and women who nurse each other. In Indian society, homosexuality is forbidden subject. Many writers have chosen lesbian relationship as their theme. Manju Kapur confesses: "I am interested in the lives of women, whether in the political arena or in the domestic spaces. One of the main preoccupations in all my books is how women manage to negotiate both the inner and outer spaces in their lives, what sacrifices they have to make in order to keep the home fires burning and at what cost to their personal lives do they find some kind of fulfillment outside the home." (Kapur 1)

Astha the protagonist in *A Married Woman* finds some kind of 'fulfillment outside the home' by having a lesbian relationship with Pipeelika. She has everything in life: children, a dutiful loving husband, middle class status and comfortable surroundings. Yet she has incompleteness in her life. At home, her parents do not consider her likes and interests and bring her up as a normal middle-class girl. Their expectations crush her individuality; she has two love affairs and also enjoys a physical relationship despite her parents' efforts to confine her to the boundary of tradition. Her parents learn about her affairs and restrict her by imposing middle-class values and force her to accept an arranged marriage with a foreign-returned Hemant who belongs to a bureaucrat family.

The novel explores the space of women in her domestic relationship. Kapur presents the challenges faced the women in their personal, professional, religious and socio-political life through her protagonist: "A woman should be aware, self-controlled, strong-willed, self-reliant and rational, having faith in the inner strength of womanhood. A meaningful change can be brought only from within by being free in the deeper psychic sense." (Kumar 17)

Kapur depicts Astha's life in the backdrop of the communal unrest in India with the Hindu-Muslim conflict about the sacred ground in Ayodhya. After her marriage with Hemant, Astha settles down in Vashan Vihar, a posh colony in New Delhi. She moulds herself into the role of a wife, daughter and mother but after few months of her marriage, she feels bored as she has to wait for long hours for Hemant's company. Astha has a strong desire for sex and physical relationship and Hemant does not seem to be aware of this fact. She is cynical about Hemant's love for her and feels alienated and dissatisfied.

She at times feels frustrated and lonely, finally making her look for a job. She joins as a school teacher which brings a change in her life. In school, she befriends Aijaz, a history lecturer and founder of Street Theatre Group. Aijaz appreciates Astha's work in school and encourages her talent in painting.

Astha constantly compares Aijaz with Hemant and finds him better than her husband as he always helps her, favours her in difficult situations and appreciates her for what she does; all this she does not get from Hemant. The friendship with Aijaz does not last long as he dies in a communal disturbance. Astha gets the news of his death and feels the pain of losing a good friend. It is during one of her activities related to the Manch that she goes to Ayodhya leaving her home and responsibilities and meets Pipeelika, the widow of Aijaz. They become good friends and are involved in the lesbian relationship. Pipeelika is a widow and feels lonely but Astha is made to feel lonely because of her busy husband who neither pays much attention to her nor spends much time with family. They later learn the boundaries and limitations around them.

Kapur makes Astha and Pipeelika turn into lesbians for their self-fulfillment, posing a challenge to male chauvinism. She also makes lesbianism a powerful component for the satisfaction of woman's emotional and sexual urges. Both Astha and Pipeelika rebel against the inequality, injustice and discrimination in the traditional socioeconomic culture of patriarchal system. Simone de Beauvoir opines: "Homosexuality can be a way for woman to flee her condition or a way to assume it. . . . Homosexuality for a woman is one attempt among others to reconcile her autonomy with the passivity of her flesh. And if nature is invoked, it could be said that every woman is naturally homosexual. The lesbian is characterized simply by her refusal of the male and her preference for feminine flesh." (431)

Manju Kapur has observed the woman's behaviour and presents Astha who crosses the traditional boundary of woman. Her relationship with Pipee does not cross the boundary. As the days pass, Pipee plans to go abroad for her Ph.D. Astha is left at the crossroads. She realizes that Hemant still loves her. She makes a mature decision and returns to her family.

II

A Married Woman is the story of the protagonist Astha, an artist, who challenges the constraints of middle-class existence. She is an educated, upper middle class, working Delhi woman. She lives with her parents in the government quarters in South Delhi. Her father is a government servant and her mother a conservative and orthodox traditional woman. Her parents bring her up with utmost care in a way a girl is expected in a patriarchal system. Her parents want her to study only to get a good husband.

Astha had dreams full of romantic fantasies during her school days. She often imagines about a romantic and handsome young man holding her in his strong manly embrace. She is carried away by her dreams and falls in love with Bunty who is an army cadet at NDA, Kharakvasala. Their love flutters and paves way to write letters to each other and make Astha daydream:

> He had glossy black hair, which he wore in a small puff over a high wide forehead. His eyes were like soft black velvet, set in pale sockets over the faint blush of his cheek. And just beneath that the bluish black shadow of an incipient beard, framing a red mouth. As she stared, steady, unwavering, he felt her gaze, looked up and smiled. His teeth were small, white and uneven, and she lost herself in them, he raised his left eyebrow slightly. She shuddered, and weakly smiled back. Thus, began her holidays. Boarding school, boarding college, as a result, he knew few people in Delhi. He took to dropping in with his sister. There was the attraction of her devotion. Day and night, the thought of him kept her inside churning; she was unable to eat, sleep, or study. Away from him, her eyes felt dry and empty. Her ears only registered the sound of his voice. Her mind

> refused to take seriously anything that was not his face, his body, his feet, his hands, his clothes. She found temporary relief in sketching him, sketches that were invariably too bad to be mulled over. (8-9)

Her romantic fairytale blossoms for a short period as her mother soon learns about the love affair and intervenes. The association with boys makes her mother Sita spy son her. Astha feels uncomfortable when she learns about her mother's intervention in whatever she does and wherever she goes. Astha's mother wants to see her daughter well-settled in a reputed family.

Sita is upset about Astha's falling in love with Bunty. Astha on the other hand does not believe in traditions and customs of patriarchy, she says, "I don't believe in all that stuff . . . and think, as an educated person, neither should you." (1) Her mother's intervention in her love affair with Bunty has a tragic end. She stops talking to Bunty and later joins college for further studies. In the college, she befriends Rohan. She starts missing classes, tells lies at home and looks for isolated places to spend time with him. She is attracted to him emotionally and physically. Rohan takes advantage of her as a pleasure-seeking commodity. She develops romantic dreams and closeness with Rohan when they go for a long drive by car. Their closeness ends when Rohan starts preparing for exams to go abroad for further studies. Astha could not imagine going abroad for studies as her father was "a minor bureaucrat who had never studied abroad, whose sole possession was 280 square yards in the wilderness beyond the Jamuna." (29) "Away to the west, where ordinary mortals cannot go, where even the words PPE and Oxford showed Astha how great the distance was between them." (29) She felt like his old Vauxhall, ugly, and useless. She knew that "it was over." (31)

Astha has become a victim of male passion. Her infatuation for Rohan teaches her a lesson and upsets her modern thinking. The relationship with Bunty and Rohan gives her knowledge about male exploitation. It also leaves her mentally and physically sick as she drifts from college to university. Astha's mother reminds her about their responsibility of getting her married. Sita believes in Shastras: "When you are married, our responsibilities will be over. And they remind her about the Shastras that if parents die without getting their daughter married, they will be condemned to perpetual rebirth." (1)

Astha's father, a bureaucrat, plans a bright future for her without recognizing her inner potential. Her mother wants to see her settled in a reputed family. Astha's modern thinking does not understand her mother's intervention in her affairs. Right from the beginning, her parents subjugate her by their traditional concepts and beliefs. Her mother always cautions her about what befits a woman and creates all types of hypes through punishments whenever she tried something fishy and "tightened their surveillance." (28)

Sita collects spoon by spoon, a sheet-by-sheet and jewellery by jewellery for her daughter's marriage and starts the search for bridegroom. But the generation of Astha is bound to revolt against parental obligation of marriage. She enters the marital phase of her life like any female, not knowing what to expect. She rejects every proposal her mother brings as she is in a dilemma about the consequences of marriage. The rejection from Astha upsets her mother especially when a suitor comes for her and she yells at her mother and says that she has just come from college, is tired and is stinking with sweat. She is not at all interested to meet the stranger. She "collapsed against the bathroom door, tears falling, crying, crying for Bunty, crying for the lack of love in her barren life, crying because she didn't want to see a dull solid man in the drawing room who advertised for a wife and asked about sports." (21)

Her mother is upset at Astha's behaviour as she does not come out of the bathroom till the suitor left. She once again reminds her about their responsibility of getting her married: "There is a time for everything. The girl is blossoming now. When the fruit is ripe, it has to be picked. Later she might get into wrong company and we will be left, wringing our hands. If she marries at this age, she will have no problem for adjusting. We too are not so young that we can afford to wait." (20)

Astha's parents try to make her understand the situation. Her mother told her, "Our Shastras teach us how to live. You will learn from the *Gita*, the Vedas, the Upanishads" (28). However, Astha does not show much interest in those texts on the pretext that her Hindi is not very strong and reacts strongly: "I don't believe in all that stuff and I think as an educated person neither should you." (1) Astha is Kapur's emancipated New Woman "conscious, introspective, educated, wants to carve life for herself, to some extent she even conveys a personal vision of womanhood by violating current social codes." (171)

After protesting many times, she finally agrees to marry any boy her father likes. Her parents convince her to get married to Hemant, the son of a bureaucrat in the Commerce Ministry, living in Delhi. He is an MBA, has returned from America and is working as an Assistant Manager at a bank in Delhi. Hemant seems quite modern: "The boy doesn't believe in dowry. Must be the foreign influence, couldn't be his father." (35) Hemant is a mixture of western and eastern culture. As Julie Myerson writes in her article: "Most of all, the even-handed and touching portrait of her marriage—the husband who genuinely cares and wants to be sexy and progressive, but is in fact the uneasy result of traditional upbringing mixed with Western education—is brilliantly done. Kapur is a generous, far-seeing writer, who knows there are no answers, no conclusions to be drawn. Maybe that's what I most admire; she thinks and writes in vivid colours, but it's the gray area—life's queasy compromises—that she furiously yet tenderly exposes."

After the wedding, Astha gets Hemant's love and comforts of life. She feels as an emancipated woman because there are no obstacles either from the parents or from the husband's side. Slowly she imbibes the values of marriage, "seems to enjoy her marital bliss as the days pass by. Astha's heart was full of love as the lake was full of water." (42)

According to Hindu philosophy, one cannot find "Moksha" without marriage. Simon De Beauvoir says: "Marriage is the destiny traditionally offered to women by society." Astha reorders her life, neatly fitting into the pattern of a daughter-in-law and wife. She dutifully moulds herself to the needs of her husband and family. Hemant comforts her with liberal thoughts about children and shows broad thinking by saying that having a boy or girl will make no difference to him: "In America there is no difference between boys and girls. How can this country get anywhere if we go on treating our women this way?" (57)

Married life seems to be beautiful to Astha as she shares her interests about poetry and painting with Hemant. Hemant praises her writing and says: "you certainly have a nice imagination" (42). Astha heard him with satisfaction; her husband was going to encourage her writing. Maybe she could become a poet as well as a painter. Her life opened up before her in golden vistas." (42)

Hemant expresses great concern towards Astha. He is a modern man who accepts the equality and emancipation of woman. As Simone de Beauvoir states: "The traditional form of marriage is now undergoing modification, but it still involves oppression, which the two spouses feel in different ways. With regard to only the abstract they enjoy theoretical rights, and are today almost equals; they are free to choose one another than formerly, they can separate much more easily. Especially in America, where divorce is no rarity; differences in age and culture between them are commonly less marked than they once were; the husband recognizes more willingly the independence his wife demands; they may share the cares of housekeeping equally; their diversions are enjoyed together: camping, bicycling, swimming, motoring, and so on. The wife does not necessarily spend her days awaiting her husband's return; she may go in for sports, belong to clubs, associations, musical organizations, and the like, she is often busy outside the home, she may even have an occupation that brings her in a little money." (2)

Astha submerges herself in the role of daughter-in-law and wife. She spent time in the kitchen experimenting with new dishes. Hemant's clothes she treated with reverence: "Sliding each shirt in his drawers a quarter centimeter out from the one above so they were easily visible, darning all the tiny holes in his socks, arranging his pants on cloth-wrapped hangers so there would be no crease. With her mother-in-law, she visited and shopped in the mornings, the memory of the night past, and the expectation of the night to come insulating her from any tedium she might otherwise have felt." (43)

Astha seems to enjoy marital bliss but one fine day Hemant resigns from the bank job and starts the business of manufacturing South Korean T.V. Sets. He is busy with his newly established business and has to go on tours for more than two days many times. He spends limited time with the family and has no time to share Astha's feelings or daily routine. She suffers from a sense of incompleteness, oppression and anguish and feels lonely. She feels suffocated with the growing needs of her family and "Always adjusting to everybody's needs." (227)

Manju Kapur depicts the gripping political situation with the same fervour and graphic detail as she describes Astha's actions and inner turmoil. Rollason says: "Astha Vodera, a school teacher with an M.A. in English, lives a comfortable, conventional Delhi Hindu middle class life, within an arranged marriage with her businessman husband, a self-satisfied materialist who sells South Korean T.V. Sets, and their two children, until she meets Aijaz Khan, a secular Muslim involved in a progressive theatre."

After a few months of marriage, dullness begins to taint Astha's life. She starts feeling a recluse at home. Astha's desire recedes: "She had been waiting for him all day, thinking of their being together, but nothing of this was reciprocated. He was a criminal destroying her anticipation, ruining her happiness." (50)

She feels dreary and distanced from him. "She was a wife too, but not much of her was required there." (231)

In her efforts to fit in perfectly in the mould of an endearing wife and daughter in-law, she at times forgot her own identity. She enjoyed the initial few years of matrimonial bliss, treading the unexpected realms of physical attraction and enjoying for the first time the joys of physical intimacy with Hemant and feels complete as a woman. But when Hemant gets busy with his business, she thinks of taking up a job. Initially her in-laws were against her taking up a job but agreed later. Astha considers choosing between journalism and teaching profession; her husband and mother are in favour of a teaching job: "Journalists have to stay out late, they have very odd hours. We must see about a teaching job. You read quite a lot." "I don't think that alone will equip me," said Astha briefly wondering whether all women are destined to be teachers or nothing. (47) Though she has never shown any interest in teaching earlier, but the desire for emancipation makes her take up job of a teacher in a public school. As a teacher, she expresses commitment to her profession.

Astha starts spending time at school and enjoys the ambience. She involves in school activities and becomes a close comrade to the principal. The principal is impressed by her hard work and hands over some of the responsibilities to her. As the days pass, Astha feels torn between her duty and responsibility; she feels that she is entrapped with domestic work and responsibilities: "A tired woman cannot make a good wife" (154).

Astha understands a married woman's place in the family to be that of an unpaid servant or a slave: "A willing body at night, a willing pair of hands and feet in the day and an obedient mouth" (231) are the rudiments of a married woman. She enjoys the time spent at school but the pleasure ends as she becomes pregnant. Hemant is happy with her pregnancy and takes utmost care of her. She gives birth to a baby girl. He tells his mother who wants the child to be a son, to be liberal towards gender and says: "But Ma,

I want a daughter. In America there is no difference between boys and girls, how can this country get anywhere if we go on treating our women this way?" (57)

Hemant's involvement in taking care of the baby and helping her in domestic works give relief to her. Astha feels comfortable as she has got all that she wants. When her daughter Anuradha is four, her mother brought in a poojari to perform a special pooja to propitiate the gods to grant them a son. However, Astha thought that the baby was going to be another girl and shares the same with Hemant who is not happy with the thought of having a girl again. Astha's happiness ends with the second pregnancy, she could see the loving and caring husband showing discrimination for boy and girl and being all Indian than being American. Manju Kapur gently digs at the Indian attitude of preferring a baby-boy to a baby-girl. Astha's answer was curt: "But Hem, I do not wish to go on trying and trying until we get a son." (68) However, Hemant's desire to have a son and his insistence that he would not stop until he has one, makes Astha dissatisfied and uneasy.

She starts experiencing the troubled marriage anxiety, isolation and discomfort again. She blames herself for all the unhappiness in her troubled relationship which results in the form of terrible headaches. She is a working woman but is denied the right to spend what is her own. This is the form of ostracization which leads to restlessness and desire for emancipation.

Astha's mother is glad when her daughter gives birth to a son: 'The family is complete at last' (68). Hemant's mother is happy at the birth of her grandson. Astha loves her motherhood and never forgot the child's first smile: "It lived on in her memory, a link between a male and her that was joyous, simple and unproblematic. So what, if it was with her two-month son" (69). She felt satisfied as it "made her feel that she had partaken of the archetypal experiences marked out for the female race." (69)

The naming ceremony of the boy is carried out on a much grander scale than that of Anuradha. Caterers came early in the morning, setting up their fires in the narrow driveway. The priests arrived for an elaborate puja and havan:

> An auspicious sign, same letter as his father said everybody, and he was christened Himanshu. By giving birth to a son on the one hand, she proves herself not "socially inferior" and enjoys the gratitude of her family members for whom the family is complete at last. (68)

Astha's second child burdens her with more work, putting an end to her happiness. "Between Anuradha's birth and Himanshu's birth, Hemant is not helpful like previously, he has changed from being an all-American father to being an all-Indian one." (70) When Anuradha was born, Hemant was loving and caring. He insisted on giving Anuradha her Sunday bath and helped Astha by sharing the household work. Hemant comforts her by saying that he had been educated abroad and seen how couples participated equally in bringing up the child. "He insisted on doing this, ideas about fatherhood are so antiquated in India." (60) Hemant refuses to help in Himanshu's upbringing as he is busy with his business. Astha finds it difficult to cope single-handedly with the problems of job and house. She toys with the idea of resigning her job but does not wish to do so: "she too had changed from being a woman who only wanted love, to a woman who valued independence, besides there was the pleasure of interacting with minds instead of needs." (72)

Like every married woman, Astha has a liking for motherhood but she does not like the preference for a son by her in-laws. She is surprised at the reaction of the family and society when they blame her after Anuradha's birth while it is an overwhelming approval of motherhood after the birth of Himanshu. Astha is disturbed by the attitude in the family but decides to push her frustrations aside and focuses on her duties as a mother, wife and daughter-in-law. She shows her multifaceted outlook in balancing the house, job and children. She wants a secure economically stable life. As an educated and employed woman, she feels she can compete with others and prove her status in society. But Hemant and his parents do not given her a chance to do that.

Astha plays the role of both mother and father for her children. Hemant's money-minting attitude towards business makes Astha unhappy. Hemant's T.V. manufacturing business, Astha's joining as a teacher, her giving birth to Anuradha and Himanshu bring many changes in her life which makes her feel frustrated. Her mother-in-law is supporting enough to say: "I am glad my daughter-in-law does not feel she has to sit at home. Till I have the use of my hands and feet I will help you, but it is my duty to point that you are going too far." (187)

Her motherly duty occupies her for some time, but very soon, boredom of routine life enters. The effort to adjust and accommodate with the problems of children, husband, servant and job make her sick with regular headaches. She feels the need for a space for herself, an urge to have an identity.

Her aspiration for companionship, to be an equal partner in man-woman relationship disappears when Hemant says: "Grow up Az, one can't be courting forever" (66). Discontentment in marital life leads to anxiety and loneliness; Astha experiences the feelings of guilt, negativity and lack of self-esteem.

She constantly struggles for recognition. In the patriarchal society, Astha's opinion on financial issues or in any other decision is not given any importance. Astha finds fault with Hemant's attitude and blames her in-laws for his upbringing. She starts learning about Hemant's attitude towards women: "for bringing up Hemant to never regard women as beings so to be consulted in their own lives." (98) Hemant does not prove to be a suitable husband nor does she become a desirable daughter-in-law.

After her father's death, Astha wants her mother to stay with her but she does not agree. "It doesn't look nice." (85) She becomes emotional when her mother decides to donate her father's books to the library. She wants to preserve them as her father's memory. Her mother and Hemant decide to donate the books to a library; her mother says: "It is Hemant's house, and he said there was no room." Astha retorts: "Then who am I? The tenant? We could have found room, we could have built bookshelves, done something, and we could at least have discussed it." (7)

She is also surprised to find Hemant not interested in keeping her mother in the house. Astha feels when she learns that her mother had sold her plot and shifted property to Hemant to re-invest it without her consent. Her mother's entrusting all the financial matters and a big part of the money to Hemant is shocking to Astha. As Clara Nubile says in "The Danger of Gender": "In modern India, the situation is still far from an ideal, liberated, democratic model. Indian women keep on struggling against the burden of tradition, against the legacy of the past and the orthodoxy of patriarchal system" (271). Astha says: "The decision taken by her mother for Hemant to carry the legacy makes her feel that can't we i.e. neither Astha nor she can manage money, since they are women?" She further says: "Really, Ma, don't you think women can be responsible for their own investments?" (97) She gets angry at her mother's decision to shift to Rishikesh for spiritual enlightenment. She visits Rishikesh to persuade her mother to live with her but does not agree.

Astha's relationship with Hemant gets dissatisfying and stifling. "She did not want to be pushed around in the name of family. She was fed up with idea of Indian womanhood used to trap and jail." (168) Ashok Kumar says about the portrayal of women characters by recent Indian women writers: "A major preoccupation in recent Indian women's writings has been a delineation of inner life and subtle interpersonal relationships. In a culture where individualism and protest have often remained alien ideas and marital bliss and the women's role at home is a central focus, it is interesting to see the emergence of not just an essential Indian sensibility but an expression of cultural displacement. Manju Kapur has joined the growing number of women writers from India on whom the image of the suffering but stoic woman eventually breaking traditional boundaries has had a significant impact." (3)

Astha's mother's restlessness, anxiety and tension is representative of "the disease of modern life." (76) She remembers her mother's words "woman is earth" (69). Conscious of man's ignorance about woman's suffering, she asserts her rights with the knowledge that "Religion is a choice as much as any other thing." (89) And the duties, responsibilities and obligations help a married woman to understand the grandeur of Hinduism. Astha does not believe that only a woman can bring purity and peace to the family. She asserts her identity through her paintings. She finds refuge in her art and also earns through her paintings.

She is depressed when Hemant squanders the money earned by her through the sale of one of her paintings on airline tickets for the Goa trip. She says: "I also earn!" to which Hemant snorts, "What you earn, now that is really something, yes that will pay for the holiday." (165) Hemant does not allow her to spend her money to buy anything of her wish. She wants to buy a carved silver box but her desire is crushed ruthlessly. Hemant says, "You must be out of your mind" (165). The tone of refusal hurts her. The male dominance is clear: "Nine thousand five hundred rupees spent on one of the worst weeks of my life, thought Astha, as she stepped into the hotel bus for the airport. She thought hopelessly of all the things she could have done with that money, of the beautiful silver box she could have possessed and admired forever. But their money spent was decided by him, not by her." (161)

Astha's agony is clear in the lines, "Please, Hemant. I am thirty-six. I need to be independent." (161) Commenting on Astha, Binod Mishra writes: "The new generation of woman delineated in *A Married Woman* evinces the split in their personalities. They are all highly educated and are accustomed to the sound and the fairies of the world. Their eyes and ears, ascertained to the ups and downs of the fast-changing world long to experiment something unusual to satisfy their suppressed ego. And in their venture to do so, they fall a prey to false temptations. These temptations distance them from their practical responsibilities and they burgeon forth a tree of detachment. The urge to lead their own lives and the impulse to galvanize them, drive them ultimately to disappointment."

Astha is a sacrificing mother. Her temperamental incompatibility with her corporate husband compels her to play the role of "mother and father" for her children. The self-fulfillment is denied and the institution of marriage collapses. Her discomfort and unhappiness lead to the feelings of guilt, negativity and lack of self-esteem. Virginia Woolf's suggestion is apt in connection with the situation of educated women: "But it is not education only that is needed. It is that women should have liberty of experience, that they should differ from men without fear and express those differences openly be encouraged to think, invent, imagine and create as freely as men do." (33) Astha feels disappointed that a married woman's place in the family is that of an unpaid servant and she has no liberty to spend her own money. She does not think that "Marriage is just sex" (275).

Astha is shocked and apprehensive when she finds a condom in Hemant's travel suitcase. He tells her that girls are often offered for the business tycoons but he never accepted them. However, Astha is not convinced. She fights back when he tries to come close to her for sex: "then what? Do I have it just because you are my husband? Unless I feel close to you I can't—I'm not a sex object, you have others for that." (224) Astha's emancipation is visible when she questions Hemant.

> Hemant relaxed that old thing. He took her face in her hands. Sweetheart, why do you upset yourself over nothing? You are my wife, I love you, and there has never been another woman for me, never. On business trips, people do not understand commitments to wife and family; they assume their clients want a good time. If I had sex, would the condom not have been used? (224)

However, the discovery of condom gave a big jerk to Astha's marital life. Its implications ran through her mind: "Who has he slept with, he who was never in any place for long, it could not be that he was in love—or had a relationship—or maybe he did. Some women might travel with him, how would she ever know? May be the distributor had supplied him with someone, she had read somewhere that women were often a part of business deal." (212-13)

It is a universally known fact that humans are sexed beings; there is sexual difference; there is sexual mystery. Authors and artists work on the human beings. Until recently both in the Western and Eastern literatures, art and movies, women were not considered human beings. As the feminist theoretician Josephine Donovan observes. "They are objects, who are used to facilitate, explain away, or redeem the projects of men . . . women are the objects, the scapegoats, of much cruelty and evil." (214) Betty Friedan's *The Feminine Mystique* questions why a woman in a patriarchal system is confined to domesticity and childcare. She observes: "For woman, as for man, the need for self-fulfillment—the autonomy, self-realization, independence, individuality, self-actualization—is as important as the sexual need." (282).

Astha finds herself in an alienated condition as her mother leaves for Rishikesh and Hemant is busy with his business. In the absence of her mother and husband, she is attracted to charismatic young Muslim Aijaz Akhtar Khan, a lecturer in History, an intellectual artist, the founder of 'The Street Theater Group.' He teaches educational theatre in the school where Astha works. After meeting Aijaz her life takes a new turn.

During vacations, Aijaz performs plays at schools, slums, bus stops, factories, streets, small towns and villages to generate social awareness. He is the voice of wisdom and sanity. He dramatizes social issues like unemployment, poverty and communalism. Astha is fascinated by the multifaceted personality of Aijaz; he makes her come out of her frustration by participating in a workshop on communalism organized by him. He encourages Astha to explore her skills and write a script for a play centered on the demolition of Babri Masjid. This earns her appreciation from Aijaz which she never experienced with Hemant. She is attracted to him and cannot help but compare Aijaz with her husband. She finds the former to be indifferent. She finds Hemant "dispassionate and taking her for granted, maneuvering homely chores, attending social get-togethers, helping the children with their homework expecting her to be a good wife. When she was with Hemant, she felt like a woman of straw, her inner life dead, with a man who noticed nothing." (287)

Astha becomes a friend of Aijaz and his wife Pipeelika who assists him in his performances. They move fast with all the explosive events that appear to affect seriously the peaceful social life of the country with the demolition of Babri Masjid. With the encouragement given by Aijaz, Astha involves in the street theatre group which comes to her school to hold a workshop. Aijaz and Hemant develop a very good rapport but it lasts for a short time only. Aijaz persuades Astha to participate in his mission. A trip to Ayodhya throws light on her potential and modern thinking. Aijaz comes close to her and encourages her to act on his theory:

> 'It doesn't matter Astha,' he said. His voice was coming at her, his eyes were looking at her, any second and his teeth would glow at her. She was married; she should not be registering these things. She shifted uneasily on the hard canteen bench, clutching her bag in her lap. 'The thing is,' he went on, 'we have to create awareness. There may be differences of interpretation, it doesn't matter. If our players and our audience think for one moment about this issue, we have done our jobs. (110)

Aijaz actively participates in the communal agitation following Babri masjid demolition and Hindu-Muslim riots. His troupe is, horrifically, burned alive by some anti-social elements mercilessly in their van one night. Astha is shocked at the news and joins the protesting crowds. The turmoil in the country deeply disturbs her.

She cannot control her tears when she watches the news. Hemant, watching her crying, loses his temper and asks her:

> 'Why are you crying?' he demanded. 'What was he to you?'
>
> 'Some murderers trap and burn a whole theatre group in a van and you ask me why I am crying.'
>
> 'This kind of thing happens all the time; I don't see you wasting your tears.'
>
> 'I can't weep for the whole world, only when it means something to me. Maybe I am deficient, but I knew him, he was always working for everybody's good, even the children loved him. And, he has been burnt to death. Isn't that reason enough?' She sobbed rocking to and fro with rage and grief. (139)

Since the establishment of the society, woman is treated as the weaker sex, denied justice, social security, economic liberation and political awareness. In this context, Simone de Beauvoir says: "The situation of woman is that she—a free and autonomous being like all creatures—nevertheless finds herself living in a world where men compel her to assume the status of the other." (167)

After Aijaz's mysterious murder, Astha once again feels lonely. She longed for companionship and love but she could not get either from Hemant. Astha could not forget the dedication Aijaz had towards society and missed his company. She involved herself in organizing processions to ensure religious harmony in the country.

Fed up by her married life, Astha shows interest in social activities. She gets disillusioned with human nature in general and politics of the country in particular. The politicians, in the guise of democrats and socialists, organize yatras for their vote banks under the pseudo-secular banner of national unity. "As for that Sampradayakta Mukti Manch, she hated it more than anything. . . . All they did was hold exhibitions, raise money, and indulge in culture nonsense." (182)

She turns her attention towards the Manch activities, which is formed after the death of Aijaz. She brings out the artist in her and paints pictures to raise funds for the political group founded in the memory of Aijaz. She goes to Ayodhya to participate in the political meeting and meets Pipeelika, wife of late Aijaz.

At home Hemant detests Astha's involvement with the Manch and tries to emotionally maneuver her in the name of children and familial duties. Even her mother-in-law looks at this disapprovingly and tells her: "a woman's place is within the confines of house not on the roads and politics is not a field where women should participate." (116)

She involves in the group activities along with the widow Pipeelika. She learns that Aijaz's death was a sectarian attack and feels empathetic towards Pipeelika. She feels drawn towards Pipeelika and an intimate emotional and physical relationship develops between the two.

In *The History of Sexuality, Volume 1:An Introduction*, Foucault traces how in the past 200 and odd years, the politico-socio structures have derived power from complex discourses surrounding sexuality. Firstly, Foucault identifies an "era of biopower" (140), which she describes as "an explosion of numerous and diverse techniques for achieving the subjugation of women" (140). Foucault shows how the feminine body was analyzed and discoursed as thoroughly saturated with sexuality. Joseph Bristow points out in *Sexuality*: This 'hysterization of women's bodies' served multiple but related functions: the maintenance of an 'organic communication' with the social body, with the family, and with children. (175)

In the patriarchal set up, the sex role of woman has been clearly chalked out. Any deviation from this assigned role is viewed with dismay and summarily ruled out and sexual practice is declared contrary to nature which has to be stopped. A woman loving woman is considered not a healthy attitude and such couples are constantly under pressure to snap their ties.

Astha spends time with adventurous and unconventional Pipee who quickly becomes the focus and delight of Astha's life.

She is slow to recognize that it is love, but slowly, tearfully, shyly, the two fall into bed, the awakening that she experiences is far more than just a sexual one. For the first time in her life, Astha has found someone who actually wants to know her: given certain circumstances, there was no aphrodisiac more powerful than talking, no seduction more effective than curiosity.

A torrid affair between Astha and Pipeelika Khan crosses social boundaries and they find solace and understanding in each other's arms. Astha finds everything in Pipee; even the society doesn't doubt the relation between women. She gives importance to her feelings rather than the feelings of her family members. Astha is emancipated and no longer feels worthless, bored or frustrated and spends most of her time with Pipeelika. This relationship is a challenge to her husband and family. Ram Sharma says: "Manju Kapur is the first Indian feminist to introduce the lesbianism and lesbian love as an important question to be discussed by the advocate of women's rights. Kapur's assertion of sexuality in the form of lesbian relationship may create much hue and cry. Kapur told in an interview to Ira Pandey about the introduction of this plot clears all confusions. This relationship suggested itself to me as an interesting means of making Astha mature and change. An affair with a man would have been the classic . . . and so I ruled it out and tried out a same-sex affair, I don't know how successful. I have been or is this based on any real-life relationship. It is as I said a writer's experiment."

Astha develops psychosomatic symptoms of stress and depression. Her slow discovery of her differences with her husband, her change from a tender and hopeful bride to a battered wife and her meeting with Pipeelika leads her to realize the other state of woman in their "familiar distress." (188)

This leads her to an immoral, rather amoral, guilt consciousness of lesbian love. Marginalized by the family, vicious social atmosphere, sheer hysteria of communalism, she is disillusioned about the empirical study of man's nature and his framing of social values. Unlike what feminists try and make us believe, females do have an amorous side to their personality. It manifests in our desire to feel loved. Astha had a strong physical desire for sex which her husband was perhaps not aware of. Astha's involvement with Aijaz may or may not have resulted in a sexual affair; the book leaves that as a mystery. Astha and Pipeelika enjoy being together; they desire each other and revel in each other's bodies. "They had been skin on skin, mind on mind with nothing in between" (303). There exists a passionate sexual union between the two. Pipeelika "closed her hands over me, and I could scarcely breathe with the pleasure" effuses Astha." (256)

The intimacy with Pipeelika grows as Astha is fed up with Hemant's mechanical and routine love and is on the verge of losing her conventional marriage and traditional family life with him. She finds pleasure in Pipeelika's association, she "felt strange, making love to a friend instead of an adversary." (230-31) the lesbian relationship that develops between Astha and Pipee fills Astha's life with fresh air, joy and vibrant health. She cannot restrain herself from telling lies. She feels every touch of Pipeelika gives her heaven's joy and she doesn't want to lose her. "She thanked God again for this love in her life, when she had thought all chance of love was over." (235) In her interview to Nivedita Mukherjee, Manju Kapur says: "It is an attempt to infuse an element of artistic and emotional coherence. Actually a relationship with a woman does not threaten a marriage as much as a relationship with a man. But when she ends up having a physical relationship with Pipee, Astha finally throws off the fear instilled in her by her parents and her husband." (59)

She attempts to go out and find herself individually in the outer world but ultimately she returns to the four walls of her house. Astha's mind is also set according to the patriarchy. In the company of Pipeelika she does not forget that she has children at home. "A large part of hers belonged to her children." (231) Every time she runs back, it is because of her children. Astha and

Pipeelika get along with one another's support for a newfound independence and emancipation. It is an unnatural relationship for both of them. Pipeelika uses Astha to fill the void that Aijaz has left.

It is a makeshift relation in the life of Astha and Pipeelika, the former is neglected by her husband and family and the latter is a widow. They feel secure in balancing the family life and satisfying their unfulfilled desires. Astha finds her true self, the real meaning of life in the new lesbian identity that gives her a coherence and legitimacy for her existence. Astha's suffering can be traced to her psychological weakness of being a single parent child. There comes a transitional phase in life and she tends to become different from traditional women and wants to adopt a new path. The change is theoretical in nature. However, rebellion demands determination and will to stand by the cause at any cost. Christopher Rollason says: "The women in India have indeed achieved their successes in half a century of independence; but if there is to be a true female independence too, much remains to be done. The fight for autonomy remains an unfinished combat." (web)

When Hemant's health deteriorates, his doctor advises him to go out of the city for some rest. Astha tells Pipeelika about Hemant's health and his summer plan, Pipee gets angry and a quarrel starts between the two. Here Astha talks as a devoted wife which hurts Pipeelika. Astha's relationship with Pipeelika comes to an end as she is not bold and strong enough to live with Pipeelika forever. Her attempt to satisfy the emotional needs is clear defiance but it is short-lived.

Although Astha is progressive and conscious of her rights, she quickly compromises to the fact that a woman's real position lies within the family. She feels disturbed when Pipeelika plans to go to US to complete her Ph.D. She cries when she has to part from Pipeelika. "I live my life in fragments; she is the one fragment that makes the rest bearable." (264) Ashok Kumar says: "Manju Kapur has exposed a woman's passion with love and lesbianism, an incompatible marriage and ensuing annoyance. With passion to revolutionize the Indian male sensitivity, she describes the traumas of her female protagonists from which they suffer" (165).

Ultimately, Astha attempts to resist the traditions and conventions of the patriarchy and rises, builds courage against the oppression and negligence of her husband. She finally returns to Hemant not because she is afraid of conventional morality, but to rule over patriarchal hegemony and to readjust herself for the sake of the family. Manju Kapur has delineated Astha's character as a woman who seeks for space in her life, and a bit more of life than tradition will automatically give her. Astha is an emancipated woman; instead of security, comfort and responsibility, she wants her emotions and spiritual needs to be recognized.

Through Astha, Kapur offers "a frontal challenge to patriarchal thought, social organization and control mechanism." (137) She has successfully portrayed the conflict of tradition and modernity through her characters. It is the feminist protest against the phallocentric patriarchal culture. The male world imposes unlimited controls on women. Kapur empowers the protagonist Astha to give a strong resistance to patriarchy by denouncing the prescribed norms of society. She resorted to a strange way of life, protested against her subordination under patriarchy by choosing the uncommon path and she survives, discovers herself and is able to attain the psychological emancipation. Astha appears "with a missionary zeal and seems to suggest that a married woman's job is not only childbearing and housekeeping but to do something more. Here Astha appears to be Ibsenite who raises her voice against the ages old customs and trends." (65)

Her female protagonists are mostly educated, aspiring individuals caged in the confines of a conservative society. Their education leads them to independent thinking. They make a dedicated effort to carve an identity for themselves. They participate in the political and intellectual movements of the day. The writer addresses many issues that are related to the middle-class women.

Idiosyncrasy of Patriarchy and Reconciliation in Jai Nimbkar's *A Joint Venture*

The last quarter of the twentieth century proved to be a milestone for the theoretical upsurge in general and creative writing in particular. Many Indian women writers like Anita Desai, Arundhati Roy, Githa Hariharan, Namita Gokhale, Shashi Deshpande, Manju Kapur, Jai Nimbkar, Shobha De held the centerstage and dealt with themes regarding the gender issues. The rise of feminist movement raised questions regarding the condition of the entire women's community.

Women began to discover themselves in the conflict of tradition and modernity and this made them feel alienated from self and society. Many writers dealt with man-woman relationship, marital discord, gender discrimination, search for identity, male hegemony and female subordination, power and sexual politics. The insight into the women's reactions and responses, problems and perplexities, the complex working of their inner selves, their emotional involvements and disturbances helped the women writers to portray a life-size picture of the contemporary woman with all her longings and aspirations, hopes and frustrations.

Jai Nimbkar's second novel entitled *A Joint Venture* was published in 1988, fourteen years after the publication of her first novel *Temporary Answers*. She made an important contribution to the Indian English short story with her *The Lotus Leaves and Other Stories*. A short story writer of sustained and steady growth during the last three decades, Jai Nimbkar is now as a mature novelist. She delves deep into male chauvinistic society and offers an authentic conflict between tradition and postmodernity. The middle-class married woman's identity crisis emerges from her works. *A Joint Venture* comes close to being as per the claim on its cover, "A truly mature novel by the author of *Temporary Answers*." It elaborates how the contemporary novelists deals with the predicament of Indian women by observing external behaviour as well as depicting the internal journey in the psychological dream of the feminine sensibilities. It reveals the women who are torn between individuality and society. The study also explores the suffering and emancipation of the career woman which is result of the patriarchal greed of power over them.

A Joint Venture emphasizes two crucial incidents which occur in the first and the last chapter respectively within the duration of a few days. The protagonist Jyoti Deshmukh's married life of twenty-five years is compressed in the opening chapter. The novel begins with the startling decision of Jyoti to leave her husband Ram's house after a happy married life of twenty-five years. Unable to understand her emotional decision to break their marriage, Ram advises Jyoti to think again and invites her to accompany him for a holiday at their favourite hill resort Mahabaleshwar. Ram thinks that spending time together will calm her down and eventually change her decision and to return to him. The novel unfolds her past life of twenty-five years in a series of flashbacks that shifts between present and past.

Jyoti is an intelligent girl from a poor middle-class Brahmin family of Pune. She secures distinction in B.Com,, topping the list in the college. Her father, who works under a doctor as a Compounder, is paralyzed by a stroke and is bedridden. The family lives on the meagre pension of his father and her mother's poor salary who works as a teacher. As eldest child in the family, Jyoti has to shoulder the family responsibility. Simone de Beauvoir observes: "One is not born, but rather becomes a woman. It is civilization as a whole that produces this creature which is described as feminine." (295)

Jyoti forgoes her studies and starts working as a clerk in a bank; she becomes the breadwinner of the family. The possibility of getting her married is further marred as she is not good-looking. She faces many rejections from the boys who come to see her. Jyoti has dreams of a loving and happy life as she has a bitter and starved life. Her parents look for a suitable groom, though not immediately. They are also aware about the dowry demands.

Jyoti's parents get a proposal from Ram who is guided by his father's friend Sripada Roa who tells Ram that Jyoti is a "capable and responsible girl, not a decorator-doll." (25) Ram visits Jyoti's place to see her and wants to marry her as he finds her different from other girls: "because of her circumstances more responsible and less spoiled than some girls from a wealthier family." (29) Jyoti also likes the proposal as Ram is from an upper-class rich family and does not demand dowry. He also says that "I want a simple wedding ceremony and we will share the expenses half and half." (27) She feels as if a dream had come true. The thing Jyoti liked the most was that he talked to her privately to know her mind about the various conditions of marriage. Her mother has many doubts about the proposal and suspects something might be wrong with the boy. As a parent, she fears that he may be impotent, but later learns that he is of sound health without any physical deficiency and she also agrees to the proposal.

Ram makes clear to Jyoti that he is from a village and she from the city but that should not make any difference. He also ensures that Jyoti is ready to give up the job. Jyoti likes Ram's attitude. Jyoti's parents are relieved by the proposal as they can marry her off without much expenditure: "She likes the direct, forthright manner in which Ram had spoken and she liked his independence. He was not one of these weak-livered young men who hide behind their parents who demand a dowry. He was not exactly good-looking, well neither was she. Any way she thought good-looking men looked effeminate." (27)

Initially, even Ram has a different opinion about marriage. The only married life he saw from close quarters was that of his parents: "The only marriage he had seen from close by was his parents, and he had not found anything in it to make him want to get married. There was no disharmony between them, but it seemed to Ram that there was very little communication." (23-24) He also feels that his parents' marriage means little at the personal level: "If that was all marriages meant, Ram thought, is there any point in getting married?" (24). He also has example of his father's widowed sister who lives with them after a miserable marriage: "She had an ill-tempered sickly husband who died, leaving her destitute, after which she had to slave for the husband's family as an unpaid servant and listen to them discuss how expensive it was to feed her and her brats." (24)

Though he has bad experiences about marriage, after meeting Jyoti, Ram feels that probably Jyoti will be as good a wife as any other, as she is smart enough to handle things. Jyoti thinks that she cannot get a better husband than Ram: "And so when she met Ram, she asked herself practically where else am I going to get an offer of marriage as good as this? And if there is risk involved in accepting it, I am willing to take it." (29)

They finally get married; Ram takes her to Mahabaleshwar which proves to be a very enchanting place for making her honeymoon a memorable one: "Everything about Mahabaleshwar had seemed touched by magic, the mountain air, the walks, the mist coming up from the valleys after sunset, shrouding everything in mystery and making her feel a little unreal, as though she existed in a make-believe world." (11)

She enjoys wandering aimlessly through the wooded hills in the loving company of her husband: "It is so nice she thought to go walking aimlessly and ends up in a place where you have probably never been before. You start down anything that looks like a train and often find that it peters out. . . . And when you do emerge into the open, it is in a totally unexpected place because you have wandered without any sense of direction for quite some time before reaching this spot." (11) Jyoti enjoys the stay at Mahabaleshwar: "She had been radiantly happy, she felt as though she had suddenly transported from a life of dreary possibilities to a paradise. As the beauty of the place unfolded under Ram's guidance, she fell in love with it, and with Ram." (17)

Jyoti feels emancipated while spending time with Ram and experiencing the new horizons because she has never been treated like this. She also likes the village atmosphere which is completely different from the city, the home of her in-laws has a pleasant ambiance. Her in-laws do not give her any responsibility of housework, all the housework is done by Atyabai, Ram's father's widowed sister. Jyoti moves freely and does farming, and also learns farming operations: "In course of time Jyoti did learn about farming operations. She supervised women workers and quickly learned to live on two levels, the individual level at which she was sympathetic, kind and helpful to them, and at professional level where all personal considerations have to be set aside in the name of efficiency and profitability." (40)

She often joins her father-in-law in farming work: "She enjoyed this quiet time with him observing, listening to his plan the work of the day, eagerly absorbing every bit of information about farming" (45). She enjoys the work in the fields as she is surrounded by the women who come to work in their fields for daily wages. Jyoti manages them well. She loves the way of her personal and working life: "That was the essence of marriage, the negation of a woman's life up to that point, and a fresh start made with new people, new ideas and values, a new style of life. This was all in the natural order of things, and Jyoti accepted it without resentment." (32)

After sometime, Ram thinks of starting seed business and makes Jyoti his business partner. He feels that Jyoti can handle the business as she has been managing the agriculture and also had experience of working in the bank. Ram does not ask her but takes her acceptance for granted. Rosemarie Tong aptly says: "Sometimes women play their roles not so much because they want to, as because they have to in order to survive economically and/or psychologically." (208) In the beginning she is surprised but soon realizes the importance of her potential:

> "Me?" she said, surprised, "having a commerce degree and working as a bank clerk doesn't exactly prepare one for running a business, you know."
>
> "But you can learn," he said, undaunted. "You know the book stuff, the concepts, you can apply them in practice. To begin with, you can start keeping proper accounts. . . ."
>
> She laughed, "Well, that's something I can help with." "Good, that's the spirit. . . With your help, I will do it. I have this feeling that together, there's nothing we can't do." (31)

Jyoti feels happy that Ram knew where exactly she fits in the business, with her educational background; she is to be the accountant and financial manager of the company. Jyoti also feels happy that she will be contributing to the business. Perhaps what she liked best of all was the way her personal and working life intertwined.

Jyoti concentrates on her work but soon feels that work has become her life. Ram works systematically and diligently. He knew all the ins and outs of the people and the business: he knew all the important people who could help in the growth of his business. He arranged parties and drinks for the cronies: "And there was of course Ram who was at the center of things, from whom these different strands flowed, He not only had amazing mental and physical energy himself, he also had a capacity to call it forth from those who worked for him." (41)

Ram does not allow his workers to be lethargic and makes them work for best results. In fact, his whole attitude to life is business-oriented. He looks at people, friends, workers and even family members with his business-friendly eyes. Jyoti adjusts herself to the situation and live up to Ram's ideas; as Ram is status conscious, she learns to dress accordingly to impress others. When he arranges parties for others, Jyoti tries to socialize with them.

Initially she does all this cheerfully out of a sense of duty and responsibility. But when the business starts growing, Ram's attitude towards the family also starts changing, she begins to resent it. She assesses Ram's character to find what he wants in life. She observes that Ram's ambition is growing day by day and he is living only for business. Now she starts feeling that she and Ram have quite different priorities in life. She wanted to live life in all its amplitude, as a person, as a woman and as a mother, but realizes that she is living not her life but what Ram wants and regrets it: "The man, the place, the job, was all part of a package which she had been given when she married. She could either keep them all or lose them all. And she had this problem basically because she was a woman." (41)

The differences arise between them and she looks for compatibility. She looks back at her married life and realizes that she has denied her own wishes and freedom since last thirty years and has been accepting all Ram's decisions: "She had been happy and comfortable in the relationship, but the fact remained that it was not subject to trial and error." (3)

Jyoti being educated helps in her husband's business but unknowingly becomes a victim of the male domination. She is an emancipated modern woman who has the capacity to think, analyze, decide and fight against all odds. She feels that she has made her life a part of Ram's life: "There was no disharmony between them, but it seemed to Ram that there was very little communication. They shared life on the principle of division of labour. He looked after the farm and the business; she was busy raising the children, running the house, looking after the dairy animals." (23-24) She is surprised to think about the depth of bitterness in their relationship. Ram shows love for her but underneath it all she felt like a dull inert mass and she resents it. Jyoti compares her marital life to a joint venture, where Ram is the decisive partner and she is the silent one. She feels like an outsider, a pretender, among the people whom she meets. She finds Ram a self-centered person. After the success in business, Ram starts dominating the people around him. He leaves the family affairs in the hands of Jyoti and does not spare any time for them. He thinks the duty of a father is only to pay for their food and upbringing.

Family life is hampered as both of them are busy in their business. As a mother Jyoti is not able to balance between business and children and that reflects on her son Pratap who is a weak and thin child. He skips the meals and does not eat properly; Jyoti concentrates more on Pratap but Ram intervenes and does not allow her to pamper the children. Pratap at times is scared at the sight of his father. Smita, their daughter with dark complexion, is bold and does not fear her father at all. Ram plays with the children but he is not soft in handling children. He very adamantly takes the decision to send Pratap to boarding school at the tender age of nine. Jyoti didn't like sending Pratap to boarding school: "I do not like to send him away at such a young age. Why cannot we wait few years?" But she had to accept it as Ram did things that way: "I do not think he is so young, many nine-year-old children are sent away to boarding schools." (92)

Children distance themselves from Ram for the way he handles them. Ram says: "God mixed up their sexes. . . . Smita should have been a boy." (91) Jyoti does not like Ram's attitude towards children, especially towards Smita. As a parent, Jyoti feels they have to be with their children at all times. She recollects an incident when Smita was attacked by the bull and hospitalized. Jyoti wanted to stay with her at the hospital, but Ram did not allow it: "Her grandmother is here, we are not leaving her alone" (117). He further says that giving birth doesn't mean that they have to be with them round the clock. "Just because you have a child, it does not mean you have to give twenty-four hours of the day to him, children are only a part of life and not the whole of it." (98)

It becomes a tough task for Jyoti to bring harmony between children and Ram. Pratap and Smita rebel and move to hostels. Jyoti regrets all the things that happen around and feels frustrated Ram does not allow her to fulfill her duty as a mother. Ram rules the family; he alone decides everything. Jyoti wondered what marriage meant: "Is it fear that keeps people married? Is that the whole purpose of marriage, to satisfy, within the frame of the relationship, all your basic needs? Does it mean that I ought to make any sort of compromise in order to keep alive in a relationship which has become untenable, which makes me unhappy?" (84) She is physically separated from her children due to Ram's one-sided decisions. She wonders if love was the basic foundation of marriage as she had believed till now: "It can't be a criterion of relationship. You can't say you live with someone because you love him. You live with someone because society decrees that people who stand in a certain relationship to each other should live." (143)

Their Triveni Seed business flourishes; Ram wants to further mechanize all operations of seed-processing. For this he organizes a 'wet' party for the reporters with to get publicity. But Jyoti does not like this; she feels that it meant dishonesty, fraud, double-dealing and hypocrisy. She wants business to be fair.

She is upset with Ram's attitude of taking all decisions by himself, whether it is about sending the children to an English medium school in Panchgani, buying a costly flat in Pune, inviting people to parties or not inviting an unwanted journalist like Krishnamurthy to children's birthday parties.

Ram takes her for granted and does not take her opinion in any matter. Jyoti is treated with respect by people, not in her own right, but because she is wife of a successful man. People are not aware of her work behind Ram's success. Even Ram acknowledges the fact that "his achievement would not have been possible without her help." (49)

Jyoti is happy working for Triveni Seeds but this happiness does not last long. She does not like the way Ram handles his business. She thinks of leaving Ram, her work, and Shirgao but she has no place to go. The man, the place, the job was all a part of the package which she was given when she married. She understands that there is no 'we' in their relationship; for Ram 'we' means 'I": "In fact, she had not consciously allowed it; she simply accepted it as the natural way. Perhaps that was the crux of life. It should be led with conscious intention, not simply allowed to happen." (80)

Jyoti has fulfilled her responsibility as a daughter-in-law, mother and wife but her endeavour at home and in the business is not recognized: "It was Ram's house, and Ram's farm and Ram's company. If she left Ram, she would have to leave all these. . . . This thought came as a shock." (107) After thirty long years of apparently happy married life, her marriage is on the rocks. She comes to the conclusion that life with Ram is a mere sham for her and nothing else. "She had lived through this sense, countless times with a tolerant smile, but this evening she found herself suddenly thinking, I've had enough. I want to get out. I am sick of it all the poses and the dishonesty, the verbal fencing which substitutes for conversation, the one-up-manship. Everything." (5)

She learns that Ram is shifting to Pune to expand his business and to establish a Seed Plant. He makes all the decisions without sharing anything with Jyoti. She feels hurt by the situation he is placed in: "Far-reaching changes not just in their professional life, but also in their personal life." (101) Jyoti decides that it is too much for her to go on living a meaningless life with Ram. She tells him that she wants to leave him. At first he doesn't understand what she is talking about; but when he realizes what she means, he advises her not to take such an important decision in hurry. He asks her to think with a calm mind.

During this period, Jyoti meets her friend Vinnie and shares her problem with her. Vinnie is shocked to learn that Jyoti wants to divorce Ram. She advises her to talk to Ram: "Jo, have you talked to Ram? Have you said to him all the things you said to me? I think you have gone on brooding and blown this thing up until it has assumed enormous proportions. Talk it over with Ram." (134)

Jyoti tells her there is no way she can change her decision; Ram loves her only in words and not in actions: "You said he loves me. What is love? Is it something you feel for someone who depends on you, or someone you are dependent on, or someone who does your bidding? Shouldn't someone who loves you be sensitive to your feelings, your needs?" (134)

Vinnie exclaims: "Marriage is funny; you spend twenty years of your life with a man twenty happy years. At least you think they were happy. And at the end of it you are left feeling cheated. What's it all been for? You make a home, raise a couple of children, there's no place for what you call love in man's scheme of things." (108)

Even her daughter Smita is smart enough to understand her mother's problem, as we know children imitate parents, Smita thinks in a more cultured way and tells her: "Either you believe what Daddy does or you don't. There is no middle ground, mummy, and if you do not, then you got to show it, not just follow his wishes blindly the way you've been doing all your life." (124)

Like an emancipated woman and having enough experience in managing things, she decides to sort her problem herself. To save her marriage, she does not want to walk on the sharp edge. She finally takes the decision to leave him for good. "I just feel I can't continue living with you, that's all" (6) is the stunning announcement Jyoti makes to Ram one evening. Ram is surprised by her decision and asks: "what have I done? Do I beat you, starve you and mistreat you in any other way?" (7) He is bewildered and tries to calm her down by proposing a trip to Mahabaleshwar. Vilas Salunke opines: "An enslaved woman's suffering; it is the tale of conscious erosion of the self of an educated modern woman who has the ability to think and feel, analyze and decide the course of her life" (121). Jyoti agrees to spend some time with Ram in Mahabaleshwar and think things over. She thinks Ram loves her and expects from him respect as an individual.

Towards the end of this phase of protest, Jyoti has a brief encounter with Aditya Rege; an engineer-businessman who tries to molest her taking undue advantage of her loneliness. Rege's behaviour indicates not only male insensitivity but also male chauvinism. Jyoti knows that as a woman she is distinct from a man; she is neither inferior to (imitation) nor equal to (protest) but distinct from Ram, so she wants to handle the situation by herself. As Vilas Salunke says: "Jyoti and Ram just do not remain characters; they become attitudes, reactions and in turn, representatives of the class they naturally symbolize, the feminine and masculine, yoked violently together in their joint adventure, their marriage in which seeds are collected, processed and marked but are not allowed to sprout into seedlings." (215)

Jyoti's idea of marriage and man-woman relationship changes. The experience she gained by managing the business makes her create her own identity. "I had led a meaningful and happy life before I met him, and I can, after." (34) Shift from Shirgao to Pune changes everything in their relationship and the seed business: "Now it occurred to her that she doesn't want to take the trouble to plant a garden here was a symbol. It expressed what she felt about the place. It was barren of growing things and happy memories." (2)

Jyoti learns from her friend Vinnie that Triveni Seeds is going bankrupt due to the rivalry with Ram's partners who wanted to take advantage of the family disturbances and cheated him by pasting "Triveni Seeds" label on adulterated seeds. Things get worse as Ram is not able to manage the business alone.

Vinnie also tells her that people think that Jyoti has left Ram because of the financial crisis. Jyoti was being blamed for no fault of hers. She could not digest the bad news about her husband and rushed back home. She found a sea change in Ram. Ram and Jyoti had expected different things from life. Ram apparently got everything he wanted while the things she knew worth having had quietly slipped through her fingers. But now the situation had changed. Jyoti is happy when Ram says. "Jo, all it does not matter you know. Not without you. You are the only thing that matters; the things do not touch the real you and me." (46) He realizes her importance and repents all that had happened and says: "But they do, do not they Ram? Only if you let them. But that's neither here nor there. I only know that I do not want to lose you. My life was one-dimensional before you became part of it. Everything worthwhile that's happened to me is bound up with you. I am only sorry that it's all been one way. I will make up for it. Jo I promise." (146)

The novel depicts the problems in marital life, the wife and husband like machines perform different roles leading their relationship to stress, distrust and hatred. Nimbkar writes: "Is it fear of this that keeps people married? Is that the whole purpose of marriage, to satisfy, within the frame of the relationship, all your basic needs? Does it mean that I ought to make any sort of compromise in order to keep alive in a relationship which has become untenable. People do live alone?" (84)

The personality traits which made Ram successful in business now make him look a little ridiculous, a little inadequate. Jyoti helps Ram in his business but is not given the freedom of making decisions. Jyoti's decision not to leave Ram does not come as a surrender or compromise. Jyoti as an emancipated woman decides to move out of the house. The separation makes both of them realize each other's importance and finally they are together as the bond of marriage is strong.

Jai Nimbkar has portrayed women's suffering without sentimentality and with such vividness that she may well be described as "the anatomist of the feminine psyche" (Swarup 10). Jyoti is representative of the middle-class and upper-middle class women in contemporary India. The novelist scrutinizes a significant and influential subject like self-affirmation, man-woman relationship, and family-feud, and has all the facts and poise of the great Indian tradition. Jai Nimbkar shows the strength of the bond of marriage in *A Joint Venture*.

Difficulties of Widowhood in Jai Nimbkar's *Temporary Answers*

Jai Nimbkar's *Temporary Answers* was published in 1974; it was the first full-length novel by the author. She was recognized as a mature novelist with her second novel entitled *A Joint Venture* published in 1988. More than fifty of her short stories were published in periodicals; *The Lotus Leaves* and *Other Stories* published by the Writers workshop, 1971, was her important contribution to the short story.

Nimbkar has written on a variety of themes in the socio-economic context of the post-Independence India. Inequality of the sexes, place of woman in the family and society, her search for personal identity, the meaning of marriage and its effect on the woman are some of the major thematic concerns of her fiction. In all her novels, the central theme is the existential quest.

Temporary Answers presents first-person narrative of an educated widow. Nimbkar's perceptive observation of Indian middle-class family is presented through the character of Vineeta who rejects a friend's offer of marriage, falls in love with a playwright, is not able to decide whether to marry him or not and finally to reach only "temporary answers."

Vineeta cannot avoid the socio-cultural milieu and faces bravely her misfortune of a sudden and early widowhood. R.K. Lele points out that Jai Nimbkar has "successfully" depicted in this novel the story of a lady doctor's love affair. The sudden death of her husband forces Vineeta, a pediatrician, to face the conflicts: her relationship with her autocratic mother, a much younger sister's interest in Vilas, her old friend and colleague who proposed to her and offered partnership in business and marriage. She tries to rebuild her life as a doctor and as a volunteer social worker.

Vineeta deals with situations she had not experienced earlier. Her experience in three distinct relationships, with her husband, her childhood friend Vilas and her lover Abhijit make her arrive at the conclusion that marriage is only a temporary answer and not a final solution to all problems. Rina Sarkar in her review said that the novel received initial approval for the author's "deep understanding of human nature, of a mature interpretation of responses" (17). A.P. Dani writes in his article "Jai Nimbkar's *Temporary Answers*: A Unified World of Transience": "Vineeta undergoes vicissitudes of relationships in her personal, domestic and professional life to realize that love and marriage, unless based on equality, freedom, trust and self-respect, will continue to be a temporary answer to her problems and frustrations." (3)

Nimbkar's protagonist is an intelligent woman in quest for her identity. J.M. Waghmare says: "Jai Nimbkar's fiction is characterized by feminism. But the world of her female characters ultimately ends not with a bang, but a whimper. The cultural condition of Indian women is, by and large, responsible for this pathetic situation." (17) The protagonists aspire to get something unique in their life and ultimately succeed in realizing their identity.

Vineeta is widowed at the age thirty. She stays at Pune with her parents after the sudden and sad death of her husband Nagendra. The novel opens with her widowhood, showing the emptiness in her life. Vineeta's father Mr. Athavale is a professor of geography in a city college and her mother is a school teacher. She is economically independent and takes responsibility of the family. Vineeta's father does not want any tension in the family and puts all responsibility in the hands of her mother. Vineeta observes the marital relations of her parents and does not want to be like them. She wishes to be an emancipated woman and not dominated by her husband.

Vineeta recollects the incident when her father was ill. She felt that he was a hypochondriac and always felt that he had some serious illness. He was very demanding and made everyone work for him: "He calls me every five minutes. He wants me to pour a glass of water so that he can swallow a capsule, he wants a book, and he wants to be dried if he perspires." (81)

Her mother spends her life in serving the family in the multiple roles as daughter-in-law, wife, mother of three children and a teacher. But if she falls ill, her husband does not bother about her or the family: "He is repelled by anyone else's illness. He simply ignores it, if he can. If I am ever ill, I don't of course expect him to look after me. But he won't even help himself." (82)

Vineeta's mother could never allow herself to be sick because there was no one to look after her: "I am never allowed to be sick. Your father, Vineeta, is a completely self-centered and weak man. But his weakness stays well-hidden because he has always had someone around to deal with crises, first her father then me. So he can always be charming and likeable. Even you, children, love him better." (103-4)

Vineeta's mother is a conservative woman who takes care of the upbringing of the children, finds fault with them in their errands and corrects them. Vineeta says: "I realized why mother was sometimes so bitter about it. . . . From disciplining us, to scolding the milkman for giving watered milk, all unpleasant situations were handled by mother." (32).

Her mother controls Vineeta at every step. She does not give her freedom to select her friends, even at the age of twenty. Vineeta feels, if she was a man, then her parents would have been liberal and allowed her to select her job and her life partner: "Mother never gave you the satisfaction of apologizing. She wanted a complete victory, and she got it only by leaving you feeling guilty. I had no right to demand that I be allowed to go out my own way." (12) The representation of her mother is complex and fraught with contradiction. Mother-daughter relations, Marianne

Hirsch finds, are particularly ambivalent, as daughters negotiate their way through "the fluctuations of symbiosis and separation' in their relationships with their mothers, in a quest for their own sense of self." (20)

As a child, Vineeta was attracted to her father because he never scolded or shouted at her, but now she realizes that her mother's discipline meant that she cared for her: "Even if mother had not been a strong and competent woman, she was thrust into a situation in which she would have had to become one. And father, the eldest son of an overbearing and autocratic father, was the appropriate husband for her." (84)

Soon after her parents' marriage, Vineeta's grandmother's died; the responsibility of the family including her father-in-law and four children fell on her mother since she was the eldest daughter-in-law. Sudhir Kakar opines that daughter is normally stronger than son: "The special maternal affection reserved for daughters, contrary to expectations derived from social and cultural prescriptions, is partly to be explained by the fact that a mother's unconscious identification with her daughter is normally stronger than with her son." (49)

Her mother's personality is the result of the conditioning of the hard life she lives. She has a full-time teaching job but simultaneously has to manage all the housework. She is not good at teaching; the students laughed at her "old-fashioned clothes and equally old-fashioned ideas." (108) It was only after her brothers-in-law completed their education, got job, and her sister-in law was married, her mother had children of their own, Vineeta says: "Since it is an arranged marriage, you could not say that each had sought a partner to complement his own personality. But once they came together, they must have intensified in each other the qualities for which they would, one day, dislike or condemn each other. If father had married a wishy-washy or scatterbrained woman, he would have been forced to assume more responsibility." (105-6)

Her mother tells Vineeta that one could not be best in everything that one does. One should not aim higher than human can achieve. "Most of us have to be satisfied with doing our little jobs in our little corners to the best of our ability." (107) Vineeta was good in studies and scored good grades. She went up to Medical College not because she wanted, but because she got good marks in her SSC exam, and naturally "took science rather than arts because it was the prevailing idea that the better students took science." (65)

Vineeta is well-educated and a doctor by profession. The family thinks that she may not get a good match as she is rather dark in complexion and not very good-looking. Vineeta always prayed to God to give her a good husband, with whom she could live a happy life. She is lucky enough to see her dream come true when she meets Nagendra at a wedding. He shows interest in Vineeta:

> It was not the sort of wedding we would ordinarily have found ourselves attending, but the groom's father was a friend of my father's and he had sent a special personal invitation. I would never have gone if I had known how rich the people were. The display of wealth at the wedding was something I had never seen before and I was miserable because we looked so out of place, so like poor country cousins. Somebody introduced Nagendra to me. He talked to me with practiced ease, made me talk about myself and seemed impressed by the fact that I was a doctor. It gave me confidence and I began to enjoy talking to him. Before we left that day, he asked me for my address. I gave him the address of a friend who was living in the hospital, because I didn't want mother to know. He said he might come and see me if he was in Pune and drop me a line if he was coming. (23)

Nagendra is attracted by her because she is not an ordinary girl though she looks like one. He also is like all that an ordinary girl would wish for in a husband. Their liking for one another blooms and paves way for a love marriage: "no it is was not an arranged marriage, though mother was pleased that I proved smart enough to make such a good marriage." (23) Vineeta's marriage takes place as soon as Nagendra puts the proposal in front of her parents; they readily accept as they cannot get a better bridegroom then him. He offers to have a simple marriage without the usual demands for dowry etc. Vineeta readily accepts the proposal as he belonged to the elite class in society, good-looking, handsome, educated, savvy and well-mannered, and held a steady job as a sales manager at Navbharat Electronics.

Vineeta is happily married to Nagendra, the courtship and honeymoon with him is like a fairy tale for her as he attends to every wish and desire of hers. They enjoy each other's company at home. He initially balances home and office very well; he does not bring the office work to home as other officers usually do, and makes himself available to her.

Nagendra is from the elite society and wishes to convert Vineeta into a high society woman. Vineeta belongs to the middle class and does not know the ins and outs of elite society. Nagendra is proud to possess a doctor as a wife and displays her as a showpiece to his friends. Vineeta feels: "He would have thought it a matter of prestige if his wife was a practicing doctor. He told me he was attracted to me because I was different from the other girls he knew, because I had a sense of direction." (22)

Vineeta does her best to mould herself; she feels that he is kind enough to marry her for what she is. She wants to enjoy, spend time with him at home, especially on Sundays. She is not happy when Nagendra decides to spend the whole day out attending a marriage. He tells her to join the trip but she refuses because the people at such social gatherings were mostly his male associates. She is not quite comfortable with them. "Nagendra had his group and the same faces turned up everywhere. I tried to feel part of them, but couldn't. Learn to be like them outwardly, but I rebel against it all." (23)

Vineeta expects him to spend the evening at home with her, but after the marriage party he goes to visit his parents. She asks him to visit them later but he shows least interest in staying back. She feels her husband to be a self-centered man who spends most of time with his friends. He expects her to obey him unquestioningly and tells her that he will never change his plans to suit her.

As the days pass, he does not show much interest in her or her problems and expects her to manage them herself. Vineeta does not have friends or family around her and feels troubled by the attitude of her husband: "You don't want me to interfere with anything. If you wanted your life to go on just as before why did you bother to marry at all?" (93) She feels frustrated and rebels but Nagendra just ignores her. Vineeta says: "So we had bitter fights. Or no, that's not an accurate description. It was I who fought, I who hurled accusations at him. He was comparatively calm because he was not really involved in the issue I fought over. . . . I was not a very important part of his life." (92)

She starts feeling lonely and resents it. "Yes I felt I gave all of myself and in return I should have all of him." (117). Many a time, she cries for being ignored by him: "I cried because it was impossible for me to reach him. I considered committing suicide. I took a lot of pleasure in imagining his shocked disbelief when he came home and saw me dead." (94)

Vineeta is a modern woman but could not reject the old traditions outright. She belongs neither to old generation nor to ultra-modern new generation. She couldn't share her experiences and feelings with her sister or mother; in a traditional marriage, the entire burden is set on the women's shoulders. Women are treated as custodians of culture. M.S. Pawar comments: "Marriage in India means marrying the husband's family traditions." (10)

After the marriage, her parents advise her to compromise in every situation including ill treatment. It is perhaps out of fear that otherwise their marriage will be ruined. Most of Indian husbands don't take suggestions from wives, especially in matters of financial management. M.S. Pawar says: "The woman, to gain her freedom, seeks marriage as an alternative to the bondage created by the parental family. The simple need to be independent becomes a demand. Looking forward to the role of a wife, she hopes that the new role will help her in winning freedom. But this decision brings her back to the prison." (40)

Indian women know how to manage their family, job and motherhood along with other responsibilities. Vineeta's in-laws were never supportive of her:

> I had thought of her as an arrogant woman who lost no opportunity to make me feel like a misfit in her family and her social milieu. She even instructed me about what clothes and jewellery were exactly right for what occasion, how expensive must be the presents I gave at weddings, naming ceremonies and such other ceremonies, how many dishes it was imperative to serve when I entertained certain people. She was afraid that I might betray my economy-minded, middle-class background and spoil the good name of her family. Nagendra said I was oversensitive and read slights and indignities where none were intended. (171-72)

Vineeta feels that it is an unequal marriage where her identity is not acknowledged. Nagendra is not cooperative at all.

One evening, Nagendra suffers a heart attack and dies. Vineeta is only thirty years old. After his death, she has to return to her parents' house in Pune and stay with them. She feels the emptiness in her life after Nagendra's sudden death. In India, culture, tradition and the socio-cultural conditions make the widow an outcast. Vineeta loses her strength to face the society. She does not dare to face her relatives and refuses to attend her cousin's thread ceremony. It is not that she suffers from having lost her husband but mourns the loss of a way of life. Her parents' home is far from being a quiet haven for a person like her in such a condition. She says: "I just don't feel like facing all relatives. . . . I did not say there was anything wrong with them. I just don't enjoy the idea of meeting all of them at once, that's all." (9)

To get solace for her troubled mind, Vineeta takes the advice of her friend Kishori, who suggests her to meet a saint. Vineeta shells out her pain to him: "The possibility of failure, I feel so empty; I don't feel capable of giving anything to others. I have nothing to hope for, to live for." (15) She gets solace after meeting the saint but she ponders over what went wrong and why. She feels as if she did something wrong in understanding Nagendra. She however is honest enough to admit that perhaps with the marriage Nagendra wanted to change over to a new kind of life. She regrets that she did not understand Nagendra: "Perhaps when he chose to marry me, he honestly was looking for a different way of life. Unfortunately, I adopted the negative attitude of resenting his way of life without offering him a substitute for it." (24) Vineeta blames herself for the happenings and thinks that if she worked and not remained dependent on him, he might have allowed her to have her own identity: "Perhaps, he was not really a strong man and he was looking for strength in me. But I was too blind to see any of this. Anyway, it's too late now for all this wisdom." (24)

Her tries to get herself an identity by starting medical practice on the advice of Vilas. She wishes for emancipation in career after Nagendra's death. In search of emancipation, she faces a lot of obstacles. She realizes that she "grieved for him because he had become necessary for her and was no longer there, that really was the essence of it." (18) She makes up her mind to build up her energy as an emancipated woman and face life bravely. She begins to take pleasure in little things like "the taste of a favorite food, the exhilaration of a cold shower, the feel of freshly ironed clothes against the skin." (34)

She tries to fill the vacuum left by her husband's death by starting practice as a doctor. She feels marriage and love are only temporary answers to avoid her loneliness. She undergoes vicissitudes in her personal, domestic and professional life to realize that love and marriage, unless based on equality, freedom, trust and self-respect, will continue to be temporary answers to problems.

The rigid norms of Indian society make her struggle a lot. She does not want to succumb to marginal status given to women. As an educated woman, she is against the blind beliefs and moves forward as an emancipated woman, she thinks over her situation again and again. She says: "I would laugh if someone had made a barefaced statement that women are inferior to men." She tries to preserve her identity. Vineeta thus overcomes the grief of widowhood. She can feel the earthly pleasure now, as she remembers her past relation with her first husband Nagendra which was an incompatible one. The thought of emancipation makes her feel that fortune has given her another chance: "Then I knew that it is the little things that mattered, that give continuity to life, what one thinks of as the big things are only interludes." (26)

Vineeta feels that her life is moving forward when she meets her childhood friend Vilas in Pune. Vilas has given up his practice as a doctor in the U.S. and has returned to Pune after a long stay abroad. He consoles her and simultaneously encourages her to make up her mind for medical practice. Her mother, her neighbours, Vilas and Kishori also insist her to find her own way out. Vineeta is well-qualified; she can stand on her own without depending on anyone. She needs support to stand for that she finds Vilas who convinces her to join him. He tells her that he owns a good building in a busy suburb of the city. She accepts the offer given by Vilas and tries to fill the void created by Nagendra's death.

She realizes her inner strength to start the practice as a doctor with a joint set up with Vilas. He picks her up from the charity centre where she works in the mornings, drives her around, and looks after her needs. Vineeta is comfortable with Vilas but does not want to be dominated by him: "I knew of course that the answer had to be yes. I might not be offered another miracle. Even if it was charity he was offering me, I couldn't offer to back at it." (25) Both enjoy each other's company as she puts her professional life under the care of Vilas: "I found it very comforting to entrust my life again into a man's hands. Vilas was the manager and the decision maker, though he went through the motions of consulting me about plans and estimates and even the remodelling and decorating." (26)

He occupies her free time as both are childhood friends who played. Vilas develops a liking for Vineeta as both are doctors by profession and are practising together. He intends to marry her and spends much of his time with Vineeta. One fine day, he proposes to her and tells her parents about his interest to marry her When Vilas says: "My offer is serious however; you must know I care for you. A great deal," (33) she says that she will never marry again.

Her mother worries about her daughter's future and thinks that the two should get married. She is happy about Vilas' proposal. Vineeta also considers him to be "a pleasant undemanding companion" and tells him that she "enjoyed being with him." (39) He invites Vineeta to his house for coffee, prepares the coffee himself and serves her in a unique way: "I thought it rather endearing .The way he set a tray and made the coffee with precision and an economy of movement. For all his bulk he was not clumsy. There was a special intimacy in being alone with him in his flat at one in the morning and I thought he would probably be a very easy man to live with." (32)

Vineeta feels that his attitude towards her is weak and fragile. He looks at her as a delicate and timid woman. She knows everything about Vilas and can sense that he dces not wish women's liberation and has an attitude of disrespect for women. Vineeta opines: "He would be the sort of husband who would treat wife like a fragile thing which requires protection, smother her with the good things in life and be genuinely baffled if she rebelled against playing the role of hose hold pet." (31)

Vineeta doesn't like the thought of being a weak woman as she was before. Now she turns out to be brave and bold emancipated woman. She is a different person all together and sees Vilas only as a friend and not as her future life partner: "I didn't feel self-conscious with him the way one does with someone to whom one has bared one's soul. The bonds of a shared childhood were almost like sibling feelings. It seemed immaterial that we had not had much in common." (24) M.S. Pawar writes: "Nimbkar portrays her widow protagonist, her awakening and her resistance to regressive pressures that come more from within than from without, because the chances for a widow to get remarried are meagre and also self-respect is at stake, when it comes to her remarriage." (152) Vineeta recovers the self-confidence that she had lost and does not want to be treated as a plaything. She also learns that her sister Madhuri secretly wishes to marry Vilas. Vineeta thinks that she will be a suitable wife for him.

Vineeta meets Abhijit Gokhale at Kishori's party. Their meeting is accidental but at the very first sight they feel attracted to each other and feel that they are made for each other. Vineeta says: "If I had not come back to Pune, if Nagendra had not died, it is an interesting game to regard life as a series of accidents and speculate on its course if one or the other of these accidents had not happened. But they all happened and so I met Abhijit at Kishori's party." (1)

They meet often and develop close intimacy and friendship. She learns more about Abhijit Gokhale who works as a professor and is a dramatist. They talk and laugh as if they knew each other since ages. "It was surprisingly easy to laugh and talk, enjoy myself. I felt like someone, who tries to bicycle after a long time and is surprised to find he can keep perfect balance." (3) Kishori tells Vineeta that Abhijit speaks to you pleasantly and listens to you with concentration. She also stresses that Abhijit may be interested in her: "He had the capacity to make you feel that he was really interested in you, in what you are saying. Perhaps writers need to have it in order to inspire confidence in people and make them talk." (5)

Vineeta also finds him to be a suitable person to marry. He is a man who has definite ideas on arts and his life. He shows interest in Vineeta, they take their relationship as true love, have respect for each other and similar views about marriage. Vineeta says, "Being with him, talking to him was exciting. But it made me feel lonely. He had strength in him, a completeness, which obviated the need for another human being." (64)

Vineeta's mother is upset for rejection of Vilas' proposal as she worries about her widowed daughter and wants her to settle down as soon as possible. She notices Vineeta's interest in Abhijit and asks her to marry him:

> Why don't you marry this professor Gokhale?
>
> I said, "I am not sure I want to marry at all ".
>
> "Don't be silly. You are not going to waste your whole life like this?"
>
> "Who says I am wasting my life? Actually I am trying to put it to very good use."
>
> "I am not talking about work. I am talking about marriage."
>
> "Why are you talking about marriage? I thought everything you have been saying about father is a pretty convincing argument for marriage."
>
> "Well, marriage has its faults, but a woman can't live her life alone. She needs the protection of a man, the security that only marriage can offer her. Even if her husband is a man she cannot respect or love.
>
> "It doesn't have to be like that, at least in the beginning. I don't want to rush into marriage and have it end up like that, either." (108-9)

Vineeta and Abhijit have a warm friendship and easy conversations flow between them which lead to intense love. Both feel delighted and fulfilled in their love. Vineeta desires for more love in further meetings; Abhijit refrains because he is careful enough not to cross the boundaries of social conventions, and he is a professor by profession. The situation is such that they cannot live without each other. In life there is always a contradiction between love and society. Love as a reality is great but society has its conventions and traditions and is directed to marriage and building up society.

Vineeta and Abhijit come face to face with the decision of marriage. Vineeta feels that marriage will be a bondage that will break their love; she fears that marriage will be less of fulfillment and more of a burden. She already has the experience with Nagendra; no one knows the pain she came across and the damage caused to her personality. At times she feels like running away from her parents' home because of their domination and the pressure they impose on her for getting married. Society always puts barriers, preventing the free flow of love, and does not tolerate the emotional union between man and woman outside the marriage.

Abhijit takes Vineeta to meet his aged mother. Vineeta is impressed by the mother who was also widowed at an early age and singlehandedly brought her son up. She still cooks food for him and eagerly looks forward to her son's marriage. Vineeta is conscious of the lonely life of Abhijit's mother: "The loneliness always hit me like an uncontrollable shaking fit of malaria; the loneliness hit me like a tidal wave, the frightening of total responsibility for myself." (70) Vineeta is impressed by Abhijit, the way he takes care of his mother and spends time with her. When Vineeta asks for Abhijit's help, he says: "of course I will help you, by loving you. You know I love you, don't you? That's only a temporary answer. That's all we have temporary answers. What more can you ask for?" (91)

An element of dishonesty creeps into Abhijit's love due to her insatiable demands for love and attention. She seeks emotional fulfillment for which she also involves in a sexual relationship with Abhijit. But she controls her emotions and decides to leave him as he also proves to be selfish like Nagendra.

She thinks that Abhijit's love is not going to help her in any way. He got fulfillment with her love; but another dimension of his life was his work as a writer; his mission in life and work as a dramatist suffers when he is with Vineeta. The realization of love being a temporary answer comes to Vineeta's mind immediately after an intimate physical contact with Abhijit. She feels that marriage like love is another temporary answer to her loneliness. Abhijit's persistent reassurance of a healthy relationship fails to restore her faith in a happy marital life. She is afraid to interact with world outside if she fails second time.

Vineeta is aware of this problem: "Perhaps, I told myself, living alone had finally begun to dehumanize me." (96) She shares her experience of interpersonal dishonesty which is the flashback to her role as Nagendra's wife. She told Abhijit: "Even husband and wife are often calculatingly dishonest with each other." Abhijit looked at her a long moment and said "You speak from experience?" She could not help but agree "Yes, I said evenly." (78)

Vineeta is intelligent enough to recognize the problem but is shocked at the turn of events taking place between Abhijit and her. Abhijit tells her that life offers only temporary answers and they should make the best of what was available. He further tells her that they cannot go on living like that: "I don't want to leave you and go away, but I have to. Vineeta, don't you see how untenable this situation is. . . . So we have practically one alternative to continue as we are. What guarantee is there then that even this won't develop into the kind of relationship you are afraid of?" (108)

He also tells her that they will never separate as their love is really deep. Vineeta feels only about the fulfillment that she gets in love from Abhijit. She clarifies to Abhijit that it would be better if they don't marry. Abhijit feels that he is not peaceful and decides to go away all by himself into seclusion where he would be able to think things over and attain peace in solitude. Vineeta is frustrated with the relationship with Abhijit as their love comes to such a situation where she is offended by his plans of living in idyllic surroundings for a spiritual renewal: "His idea of going and living in idyllic surroundings for a spiritual renewal still sounded strange." (160)

Vineeta feels loneliness and her internal spiritual struggle is an exhausting and nerve-breaking experience. She develops an intense headache as she does not have any clue about Abhijit's whereabouts and thinks: "but didn't I make any difference? Didn't he achieve mental peace and balance through me? Isn't that the whole idea of marriage?" (160) She finds herself in the same situation as when she lost Nagendra; now she feels to be losing Abhijit: "I felt catapulted back in time—Abhijit became Nagendra. I felt sick. What is love; I thought a struggle to own another's soul." (160)

Vineeta hates Abhijit's mean mentality and feels sick in her soul. She thinks he has gone away to strengthen his mind and also to strengthen her through his separation. She realizes no meaningful communication is possible until she realizes her real self. "It was no use sending out messages. I stood inside an impenetrable rock wall and the messages only rebounded. They never reached the living, laughing world outside." (167)

Vineeta realizes that she is looking at love in a self-centered way: "I was only marrying because I wanted to escape from the world, escape from myself. Now that I knew I was running away from myself, I would have to stop running." (167) She decides to tell Abhijit to allow her to deal with her problems. Obviously she wants to grow up, but is not sure what the consequences of such growing up would be: "I thought, when he comes back, in his own time, I would be able to tell him that I loved him. Perhaps." (173)

> I said: "Sometimes I wish we could remain suspended in this relationship. where I still have some freedom. Don't you think marriage will take away your freedom? Not in the sense you mean. But emotional dependence does take away freedom, doesn't it?" (176)

She wants a chance to deal with her problems in her own way. Abhijit must trust her even if it means not uniting in marriage. She is frustrated and tells Abhijit: "Abhijit do you understand? You must go away. You must let me deal with my problems in my own way. You must trust me." (173) The story ends with Vineeta sending Abhijit away and with the word "Perhaps" pregnant with all possibilities. If he comes back as a fully integrated person, as she expects him to, she will be ready and strong to receive him and then they will unite in love adding strength to strength.

After analyzing different aspects of marriage, Vineeta comes to the conclusion that marriage is only a temporary answer if there is no equality. Marriage is a social necessity, for without it society will die out. Man and woman would remain incomplete and unfulfilled. The final decision of Vineeta and Abhijit, not to consummate their love in marriage, but to break up the relationship, is a result of much reflection on the part of both of them. They do so because they realize that marriage is only a limiting factor, "a temporary answer", for real and deep love. In the course of this saga of love between two intimate souls, Vineeta's previous marriage with Nagendra plays a crucial role. It is not merely the background of Vineeta's emotional and psychological makeup but it serves, as a powerful contrast. She manages to break the tradition of India that shuts the widow within the four walls to live a mournful life. Her emancipated life paves way to take a right decision after lots of ups and downs in her life.

She wants to live her life with the full potential of her femininity. She protests against the social constraints that restrict her; she makes a conscious choice and rejects marriage, without giving up on man-woman relationship. Vineeta's predicament is of a common woman in contemporary Indian society. The novel ends with breaking the relationship with Abhijit and asking him to "let her deal with her problem in her own way." (221)

The character of Vineeta becomes intriguing. She is certainly not looking for total emotional independence, which will spiritually liberate her. Her dilemma makes her introspective. The apparent philosophy regarding the nature of love is result of Vineeta's deep, brooding and concrete experience. In the end, we have an image of Vineeta "feeding on" herself. Love, Vineeta feels, fails to break the barriers of self; on the contrary, it makes one run away from oneself. Finally, a feeling of nausea overcomes her. Her marriage to Abhijit, thus, becomes conditional:

> Anything less than an equal relationship was not enough must not be made to do. We must stand alone, complete in ourselves, before

> we could meet in marriage. I could not remain lame, crippled, only half a person and expect him to always lend my support, the illusion of wholeness. . . . Any acceptance of marriage must be conditional on my being able to translate this knowledge into reality. There was no other way. (220)

Vineeta, in her quest to be independent and complete, realizes that marriage is only a temporary answer to her loneliness. Derek Antao appreciates the novel mainly because it traces the process of self-realization on the part of Vineeta. She arrived at this conclusion after experiencing three distinct relationships and involvements with three different members of the male species: her husband, her childhood friend Vilas and her lover Abhijit. A.P. Dani, in his article "Jai Nimbkar's *Temporary Answers*: A Unified World of Transience" writes: "As a widow trying to encounter and reconcile with her misfortune, she is unable to choose for her life partner again." (3)

She represents the assertive woman who is torn between age-old traditions and a feeling of domestic security. She is passive through the transition of old cultural modes to the neo-modern one. In the beginning she surrenders to the tradition as a typical traditional woman but as she matures, she chooses to live life according to her own wish.

Vineeta represents the modern-day intellectually strong woman with a different vision to perceive freedom in life. At first, being a widow, she has no identity, because a widow is an outcast in Indian society. She aspires to have control over herself because she knows it is necessary to have control over the world. She confronts her loneliness and alienation with courage after her husband's death.

Through Vineeta, Jai Nimbkar delineates the struggle of the present age middle-class, educated, modern bold women. When marriage fails to provide them freedom, equality and respect, they become restless and seek dissociation from their immediate relations. In fact, in India marriage is a promised land for an Indian woman to fulfill her dreams.

Jai Nimbkar's women characters are determined to have social change. First, they want to realize their identity. Secondly, they are ready to rebel against all the norms which come in their way of getting respect from society. Thirdly, they do not think that they are inferior to the male. These three aspects are the ways to destroy the patriarchy. Economic independence, which the protagonists have, is the basic requirement of women's empowerment. Physical violence, sexual abuse and mental torture are realities of the present society; with intelligence, emancipation and education, women can change the social condition and empower themselves. Vineeta comes to the conclusion that marriage for her is not a solution to get rid of her loneliness. She is intelligent and not meek or weak.

Jai Nimbkar's protagonist is unique, with an integrated personality. They do not want to depend on men; they can very well step out of the rigid sex roles assigned to them. Subhash Chandra opines: "They carve out their own niche in the professional competitive world of advertising and acquire all that is necessary to live an independent life with no man to dictate terms." (2)

Marriage is an important aspect of life; both the genders have equal share of responsibility, mutual trust and emotional attachment for each other. However, the meaning of marriage is quite different today. It is inequality of sexes, subjugation of the female, loss of freedom and respect. The husband's house becomes the new home of the bride where she should live with happiness and contentment. Society often sees the young wife as an unpaid servant who is denied her rights as a person and is ill-treated by her in-laws. The present-day feminism is viewed as a humanistic philosophy, which seeks to challenge, change and destroy patriarchal hierarchy but it aims a balanced relationship between man and woman. They reject male domination and want to spend life without any restrictions. Vineeta as a wife is not portrayed in the pativrata mould.

That marriage as an institution favours men more than women is the thematic concern in all Jai Nimbkar's novels. G. Hampamma, in her article "Self Victimization in the Shorter Stories of Jai Nimbkar" writes: "Jai Nimbkar's characters are torn between a search for an authentic existence and the limitations of the human situation that prevent them from such realizations." (5)

Jai Nimbkar in this novel depicts emancipation and quest for female identity. The age-old Indian traditions and norms always keep women under the custody of men which is apparently to make her life safe and smooth. But on the other hand, it makes woman play a slavish role with the dependence syndrome. The modern woman knows that equal status with man is her right and she is ready to fight for it. Jai Nimbkar offers confidence and affirmation of the emancipated women who are urban, educated and professionally self-respecting, dignified and capable to handle any critical situation without male protection.

Traditionally man has been regarded as protector but Jai Nimbkar's female characters reject this attitude. They have courage to change the situation in their lives. The women characters get their self-identity, yet they are also careful not to root out the old foundations. They know that the roots are important.

Women in society have developed womanly instinct, as she is also a person more than a woman. Claiming freedom is her right in the independent country. Jai Nimbkar's female characters, instead of believing only in the "compromise and replacing into tame domesticity for the sake of security and comfort", protest against the stereotype norms.

The feminist viewpoint in these novels is not Western; it is typically Indian. This defines woman as an equal member of the society and a complement to man but not a rival. Through this novel, it is also observed that there is depiction of generation gap and its adjustment problems with the age-old traditions.

Jai Nimbkar's novels advocate many patterns of feminism encompassing agitation for equality, sexual autonomy and self-determination. Her female protagonists represent young women of third world countries who can identify their problems and needs.

Conclusion

Manju Kapur perceives the position of women in a patriarchal society and emphasizes on their emancipation in her novels. The dominant themes in her fiction include marriage, mother-daughter relationship, husband-wife relationship, separation, lesbian and extramarital relationship. She explores the lives of women who live and struggle in the oppression of a closed society. She depicts the intellectual starvation, domestic domination, physical abuse and lack of personal freedom of women.

Difficult Daughters is the story of an innocent young girl caught between sentimental attachment to family and longing for education. Hailing from a conservative Punjabi family from Lahore, Virmati falls in love with a married man who is also her teacher. Set against the backdrop of Indian struggle for independence from the clutches of British Raj, the novel presents Virmati's struggle for emancipation, self-realization and self-identification. Ida, the narrator, travels to Amritsar, to explore her mother's struggle for emancipation and her relationship with mother.

The novel depicts mother-daughter relationship in three generations—Kasturi, the mother of Virmati and maternal grandmother of Ida, Virmati, the protagonist, and Ida, a childless divorcee who is Virmati's daughter. These women struggle, and search for their identity in the male-dominated society. Virmati, the eldest of eleven siblings does not get a chance to enjoy her childhood. At the tender age, she is left with responsibilities of household chores because of her mother Kasturi's incessant pregnancy. Virmati craves for her mother's love and affection, waits for some gesture to know that she was special for her, but her mother never shows any affection towards her.

The poor girl does her best to help her mother and at the same time pursues her studies. The work at home does not allow her to excel in her studies. She looks up to her cousin Shakuntala who has done M.Sc. Shakuntala encourages Virmati to continue her studies.

Virmati falls in love with Harish who is her tenant and an America-returned Professor. The affair leads to her pregnancy but she aborts it as she does not want to bring shame to her family. Harish enjoys the dual roles of being husband to Ganga and lover to Virmati. He wants Virmati for the pleasure and Ganga to take care of his home. Virmati with the help of his poet-friend finally marries Harish but ends up with dissatisfaction in married life. She is second wife to Harish who does not leave Ganga.

Manju Kapur portrays early twentieth-century Punjabi life and effectively captures the position of Indian women in joint families under patriarchal control. Her protagonist Virmati, in search of identity, depicts the conflict of tradition and modernity. Virmati considers education to be a tool to achieve her identity. Education enables women to realize the nature of subjugation, marginalization and suppression and helps find effective ways to acquire individuality and emancipation.

A Married Woman depicts the struggle for autonomy and empowerment in a patriarchal family. The struggle to gain control of the disputed Ayodhya temple, the destruction of Babri mosque parallels Astha's emotional turmoil. This novel is a narrative of a woman in an incompatible marriage and the contemporary political turmoil is its historical context.

Astha undergoes profound changes against the backdrop of an India that is also evolving. There is a shift in values and women have started acknowledging themselves the co-equals of men. Astha is an educated, upper middle-class, working Delhi woman. She is denied the freedom to act and choose by her parents and she struggles to come to terms with her identity in the society. In search of identity, she forges many new relationships.

She represents the upper-middle-class educated woman who, although financially independent, is still facing the problems of adjustment between the old and the new, between appearance and reality and between theory and practice. It explores the space of such women through Astha and boldly presents a new perspective. (Gunjan 97)

Astha is married to America-returned Hemant who is all-American in the beginning but later turns out to be all-Indian when Astha conceives for the second time. He insists on having a male child. Astha hates the discrimination he shows between genders and is frustrated by Hemant's attitude towards women. He gets busy with his newly started business and ignores the family. Astha has to look after the children, in-laws and the whole family. She searches for peace and finds it in a school where she starts working. There she befriends Aijaz, a fellow teacher. Astha is appreciated by him for the talent she has and develops interest in him. But the interest does not last long as Aijaz dies in the communal turmoil. She develops a lesbian relationship with Pipee, Aijaz widowed wife, which is against the social norms. She finds solace in Pipee's company and spends most of the time with her. She neglects the family for a period of time as she does not get attention from her husband or in-laws. Pipee carves a better future for herself and goes abroad to pursue her Ph.D. Both Astha and Hemant realize the importance of the family and are united at the end.

In both the novels, patriarchy plays an important role in upbringing of the women characters and shaping their attitude to life. In the case of Virmati, Swarnalata and Shakuntla show her the path to emancipation and identity. In *A Married Woman*, Astha looked up to Pipeelika, a liberated woman who lived alone and married a Muslim going against the family and society. Pipeelika is a bold woman who carries the mission after her husband Aijaz's death without any apprehensions. Pipeelika's assertion of emancipation attracts Astha.

Manju Kapur's female protagonists utilize every opportunity that comes their way. They are strong individuals but imprisoned by conservative society. Education leads Virmati to independent thinking. Astha is marginalized in her own family. She takes up a job to overcome stress and depression. At the end of the respective novels, Virmati and Astha are emancipated women. They are the trendsetters who challenge the existing socio-cultural patriarchal system and boldly negotiate for their independence and a respectable place in society.

Manju Kapur shows the dilemma of women who carry the burden of being female as well as added responsibility of their families. In the traditional and social environment of the novel, mothers consider marriage the ultimate goal for women. They become a part of the political and intellectual movements of the day. Manju Kapur presents the changing image of woman; moving away from the traditional presentation of enduring woman, she presents assertive and ambitious women who make society aware of their demands and are successful in self-expression.

Jai Nimbkar's *A Joint Venture* is the story of Jyoti who comes from a poor family and marries Ram, who is rich but stays in a village. Jyoti happily adjusts in the village atmosphere. She helps her husband to set up the Triveni seed business but he does not give much importance to her. He ignores her in taking decision in naming their children and sending them to boarding school etc. She realizes that marriage may not offer the best of all possible worlds to a man or a woman, for neither a man nor a woman is complete in himself or herself. They need each other biologically and emotionally to develop a harmonious relationship. Jyoti sees her husband expecting different things from life and almost achieving everything he wanted. But it is otherwise with her. She knows that she is neither inferior, nor superior, but distinct from Ram. She emerges as a mature woman. The experience she has at her in-laws' house and in the Triveni Seeds business makes her decide to leave Ram after thirty years of her marriage.

However, Nimbkar does not take the rebellion against the male-dominated world to its bitter end. When Jyoti learns about the losses suffered by her husband in business, she goes back to support him. Ram also realizes her importance and changes. Jai Nimbkar focuses on the tradition and the bond of marriage in the Indian context. Jyoti's emancipation gives her confidence; she learns to take decisions. She knows that she can retain her identity and assert herself even when she continues to live with Ram.

Vineeta, the protagonist in the *Temporary Answers*, finds marriage to be a temporary answer to life's problems. She loses her husband at a young age and learns to face the world alone without male support. She is a well-qualified doctor but her husband Nagendra never asked her to work. Vilas, her childhood friend, supports her to start the practice and intends to marry her. However, she likes him only as a friend. Her life with Nagendra was an example of male-domination in Indian society. All the time, she had to adjust and mould herself according to her in-laws and husband Nagendra. Though she is impressed by Gokhale, she refuses to marry him because of the difference in their thinking. Vineeta comes to the conclusion that marriage is only a temporary answer to avoid loneliness. The novel focuses on the patterns of male-domination and woman's struggle for liberation from the rigid norms of Indian society.

Through the characters of Vineeta and Jyoti, Jai Nimbkar throws light upon the woman breaking the traditional bonds and becoming an emancipated woman. They come to the conclusion that marriage alone is not the solution for their problems they are many other things to achieve in their life. They also learn to lead an independent life and have their own identity.

Today women have been given bigger roles to play in the society. They are entrusted with more responsibility than their male counterparts. This positive step will lead women to a direction that will see the dawn of real freedom. Amar Nath Prasad observes in this context: "Women are no longer flowers of the pot for only decoration; rather they are fragrant flowers of the open garden diffusing aroma to all comers, braving the storms and rain" (Gunjan 98).

In such a scenario her journey from 'margin' to the 'centre' becomes even more challenged. With the evolution of society, change is palpable. Manju Kapur's *Difficult Daughters and A Married Woman* and Jai Nimbkar's *A Joint Venture* and *Temporary Answers* present protagonists who break the patriarchal domination and the social rigid norms and emerge as emancipated women.

Bibliography

Agarwal, B R. "Indian English Literature and the Crisis in Value System: A Study of *Difficult Daughters* by Manju Kapur," *Indian Fiction in English: Roots and Blossoms*. I. ed. Amarnath Prasad and Nagendra Kumar Singh. New Delhi: Sarup, 2007.

_____ and M.P. Sinha. *Major Trends in the Post-Independence Indian English Fiction*. New Delhi: Atlantic, 2003.

Agarwal, Malti. "Manju Kapur's *Home:* A Chronicle of Urban Middle Class in India," *Impressions: Bi-Annual E-Journal of English Studies*, No. 1, Jan. 2007.

_____, ed. *Contemporary Indian Writing in English: Critical Perceptions*. New Delhi: Atlantic, 2005.

Ahmad, Nadia. "'Cracking India': Tradition versus Modernity in Attia Husain's *Sunlight on a Broken Column* and Manju Kapur's *Difficult Daughters*," *The Road to Baghdad, or Traveling Biculturalism: Theorizing a Bicultural Approach to Contemporary World Fiction*, ed. Gonul Pultar. Washington: New Academia, 2005. 199-218.

Akbar, Arifa. Rev. of *Custody*. *The Independent*, 11 March 2011.

Alterno, Letizia. "Shreds of Indianness: Identity and Representation in Manju Kapur's *The Immigrant*," *Post Liberalization Indian Novels in English: Politics of Global Reception and Awards*, ed. Aysha Iqbal Viswamohan. London: Anthem Press, 2013. 77-86.

Anagol, Padma. *The Emergence of Feminism in India*, 1850-1920. England: Ashgate, 2005.

Anand, T.S. "*Paro* A Psychological Approach," *Indian Women Novelists.*, ed. R.K. Dhawan, vol. 6. New Delhi: Prestige, 1993.

Anderson, Margaret. *Thinking about Women: Sociological Perspectives on Sex and Gender*, New York: Macmillan, 1993.

Archna and Shweta Nigam. "A Woman's Struggle for Self in Man's World with Special Reference to Manju Kapur's *Difficult Daughter*," *Rise of New Woman: Novels of Manju Kapur*, ed. Ram Sharma. 101-13.

Armstrong, Isabel, ed. *New Feminist Discourses: Critical Essays on Theories and Texts*. New York: Routledge, 1992.

Bala, Suman, "The Mother-Daughter Conflict in Manju Kapur's *Difficult Daughters*," *in Indian Writing in the New Millennium*, ed. R.K. Dhawan. New Delhi: IAES, 2000.

Balakrishnan, Anita. "Marriage, Tradition and Autonomy: The Quest for Self-Discovery in Manju Kapur's *A Married Woman*," *South Asian Review*, 25. 2. Dec. 2004. 104-12.

Banerji, Mithu. "Lesbian Passion Forged in a Land of Turmoil," Rev. of *A Married Woman*. *The Observer*, 23 Feb.2003.

Barche, G.D. "Facets of Feminism in Indian English Fiction," *Indian Women Novelists*, ed. R. K. Dhawan. Vol. 1. 127-34.

Basu, Chitralekha. "A Meeting of Minds" Rev. of *A Married Woman* by Manju Kapur. *The Times Literary Supplement*. February 2003: 23.

Bernard, Jessie. "The Husband's Marriage and the Wife's Marriage," *Gender: A Sociological Reader*, ed. Stevi Jackson and Sue Scott. London: Routledge, 2002.

Bharucha, Nilufer E. and Vilas Sarang. *Indian-English Fiction 1980-90: An Assessment*. Delhi: B. R., 1994.

Bhatnagar, Manmohan. *Feminist English Literature*. Delhi: Atlantic, 1999.

Bhatt, Indira. "Marriage::The Summum Bonum of Woman's Life: A Study of Manju Kapur's *Difficult Daughter's*," *Indian Women Novelists in English*, ed. Amar Nath Prasad. New Delhi: Atlantic. 2001.

Blanco-Carrión, Olga. "Framing Interpersonal Violence in *A Married Woman*," *India in the World*, ed. Gámez-Fernandez et al,.143-65.

Boehmer, Elleke. "'First realize your need': Manju Kapur's Erotic Nation," *Alternative Indias: Cultural Diversity in Contemporary Literature in English*, ed. Peter Morey and Alex Tickell. Amsterdam: Rodopi. 2005. 53-70.

Borate. T.S, 1995, "Jai Nimbkar's *A Joint Venture*: A Study in Feminine-Feminist-Female Consciousness", *Indian Women Novelists*: R.K. Dhawan, vol. 3-4, 84.

Butler, Judith. *Gender Trouble: Feminism and the Subversions of Identify*. New York: Routledge, 1989.

Chakravarti, Jaya. "A Study of *Difficult Daughters* and *A Married Woman*", *Novels of Manju Kapur*, ed. Ashok Kumar, 53-62.

Chandra, N.D.R. *Modern Indian Writing in English: Critical Perceptions*. New Delhi: Sarup, 2004.

Chandra, Subhash. Rev. of *A Married Woman. Intersections: Gender, History and Culture in the Asian Context*, 14, Nov. 2006.

Chauhan, Vibha. S. "Women, History and Fiction: Kapur's *Difficult Daughters* and Baldwin's *What the Body Remembers*," *Desert in Bloom: Contemporary Indian Women's Fiction in English*, ed. Meenakshi Bharat. New Delhi: Pencraft International. 2004.

Chhikara, Mayur. "Manju Kapoor's *Difficult Daughters*—A Saga of Feminist Autonomy and Separate Identity," *Language in India*, 10.7, July 2010. 188-95.

Chotai, Nutan. "Changing Faces of Women in Manju Kapur's *Home*," *Contemporary Fiction: An Anthology of Female Writers*, ed. Vandana Pathak, et al. 127-34.

Choubey, Asha. "Mothers and Daughters: A Comparative Critic of *Fasting Feasting* and *Difficult Daughters*," *Indian Writing in English*, ed. Rama Kandu. New Delhi: Atlantic, 2003.

Choudhuri, Sucheta Mallick. *Transgressive Territories: Queer Space in Indian Fiction and Film*. Ph.D. thesis, University of Iowa. 2009.

Chowdhury, Anupama. "Manju Kapur's *Home*: A Feminist Reading," *The Indian Journal of English Studies*. 14. 2008.

Cixous, Helen. "Sorties," *Modern Criticism and Theory: A Reader*, ed. David Lodge and Nigel Wood. New Delhi: Pearson, 2015.

Cookie, Maini. "Daughter's Labour of Love," Rev. of *Difficult Daughters. The Tribune*, 10 Jan. 1999.

Coopsammy, Madeline. Review of *The Immigrant* by Manju Kapur. *Prairie Fire Review of Books*, 11. II 2011.

Dani, A.P, "Critical Essays on Commonwealth Literature: Jai Nimbkar's *Temporary Answers*: A Unified World of Transience", 89.

Das, Bijay Kumar. *Postmodern Indian English Literature*. New Delhi: Atlantic, 2010.

Dass, Veena. *Fiction of the Nineties*. New Delhi: Prestige, 1994.

Devika. "Disastrous synthesis of Desire and Duty in Manju Kapur's *Difficult Daughters*," *Studies in Women Writers in English*, 5 Ed. Mohit Kumar Ray and Rama Kundu. New Delhi: Atlantic, 2006.

Desai, Anita. "Home is where the ghosts are," Rev. of *Home. The Sunday Times* (London), 16 Apr. 2006.

Dhawan, R.K, ed. *Indian Women Novelists*. 18 Vols. New Delhi: Prestige, 1991, 1993, 1995.

Donovan, Josephine. "Beyond the Net: Feminist Criticism as a Moral Criticism," *Twentieth Century Literary Theory*, ed. K.M. Newton. London: Macmillan, 1997, 211-15.

Dwivedi, A.N. "Manju Kapur's *Home:* A Feminist Reading," *Novels of Manju Kapur: A Feministic Study*, ed. Ashok Kumar. New Delhi: Sarup, 2010, 38-45.

Dwivedi, O.P. "The Glorification of *The Second Sex*: A Quest for Female Consciousness in Manju Kapur's *Difficult Daughters*," *Novels of Manju Kapur: A Feministic Study*, ed. Ashok Kumar, 31-37.

Fax, Jane. *Postmodernism and Gender Relations in Feminist Theory*, ed. Kemp et.al. New York: OUP, 1997.

Forbes, Geraldine. *Women in Modern India*. New York: Cambridge University Press, 1996.

Foucault, Michel. "The History of Sexuality," An Introduction. Trans. Robert Hurley. New York: Random House, 1978.

Freud, Sigmund. "The Question of Lay Analysis", trans. N. Proctor-Gregg. London: Imago, 1947.

Futehally, Laeq. Review of *The Legacy and Other Stories* by Shashi Deshpande. *Indian Book Chronicle*, Jan. 1982.

Gámez-Fernández, Cristina M. and Antonia Navarro-Tejero, ed. *India in the World*, Newcastle-upon-Tyne: Cambridge Scholars Publishing, 2011.

Ganapathy, Doré and Geetha. "Impossible Reconciliation in Manju Kapur's *Difficult Daughters*," *Commonwealth* Dijon, France,1. 23, 2000. 35-42.

García-Arroyo. "The Normative Patriarchal Family as a Conflictive Zone: A Reading of Manju Kapur's Custody," *Muse India on-line journal*, 41, Jan.-Feb. 2012. .

Ghosh, Arpita. "Women, Education and the Indian Scenario: A Study of Manju Kapur's Novels," *International Journal of English and Literature*. 3.2 (June 2013): 15-22.

Ghosh, Sushweta. "*A Married Woman*, with a Lesbian Lover," desitalk. newsindia-times.com/2002/12/20/arts20-lesbian.html20Dec.02.

Gnanamony, S. Robert. 'Rationale of Sexual Diversity in Manju Kapur's *A Married Woman.' Literary Polyrhythm's: New Voices in New Writings in English*. New Delhi: Sarup, 2005.

Green, Gayle, *Changing the Story; Feminist Fiction and the Tradition*, Indiana UP: Bloomington and Indianapolis, 1991.

Gupta, G.S. Balarama. "Indian English Women Short Story Writers: An Overview", *Vikram Journal of English Studies*, Vol. 1, 1993. 41.

Gupta, Poonam Rani. "Breaking the Tradition of Silence: A Study of Manju Kapur's Novels" *Rise of New Woman: Novels of Manju Kapur*, ed. Ram Sharma. 9-16.

Hampamma. G, "Self Victimization in the shorter fictions of Jai Nimbkar", *Research Spectrum:* 2 11, 2011. 4.

_____, "Mother Figure in Short Stories of Jai Nimbkar", *The Criterion*, 12, 2013.

Hirsch, Marianne, *The Mother/Daughter Plot: Narrative, Psychoanalysis, Feminism*," Bloomington and Indianapolis: Indiana, University Press, 1989, 20.

Irigaray, Luce. *This Sex Which Is Not One*. Trans. C. Porter and C. Burke. Ithaca: Cornell University Press, 1985.

Ishwar and Balasaheb Wakde. "Women's Suffocation and Struggle for Independence in Manju Kapur's *A Married Woman*", *Variorum, Multi-Disciplinary e-Research Journal*, 2, 2 November 2011.

Iyengar, K.R.S. *Indian Writing in English*. New Delhi: Sterling, 1985.

______. *The Women Novelists Indian Writing in English*. New Delhi: Sterling, 2007.

Jadhav, B.S. and R.S. Nitonde. 'Defiance in the Novels of Manju Kapur.' *Reflections*. 10. 1-2. Jan.-July 2011.

Jandial, Gur Pyari. "Evolving a Feminist Tradition: The Novels of Shashi Deshpande and Manju Kapur," *The Atlantic Literary Review* 4.3, Jul.-Sept. 2003. 108-28.

Joshi, H.M. *Traditional and Contemporary Ethics: Western and Indian*. Bhartiya Vidya Prakashan: Delhi.

Joshi, P.G. *Shashi Deshpande's Fiction: A Study in Women Empowerment and Post-Colonial Discourse*. New Delhi: Prestige, 2003.

______. Review of *A Joint Venture*: The Indian P.E.N, 50. 1989.

Juneja, Anita. "The Predicament of Indian Women in *Difficult Daughters*," *Poetcrit*. 20. 2. July 2007. 60-70.

Kabir, Ananya. "Abuses of Authority: English Literature, Colonial Pedagogy, and Shakespeare in Manju Kapur's *Difficult Daughters*," *Upstart Crow: A Shakespeare Journal*, 21.2001. 127-37.

Kapur, Manju. *Difficult Daughters* India: Penguin, 1998.

_____. *A Married Woman*. London: Faber and Faber, 2003.

_____. *Home*. New Delhi: Random House India. 2006.

_____. *The Immigrant*. New Delhi: Random House 2008.

_____. *Custody*. Noida: Random House. 2011

_____. *Brothers*, Penguin Random House India. 2017

_____, interviewed by Anjana Rajan: "Seeds of Hope," *The Hindu*. 5 October 2008.

_____, Interviewed by Farhad J. Dadyburjor. *DNA*. 22 March 2006.

_____, interviewed by Ira Pande. *The Hindu*. 5 January 2003.

_____, Interviewed by Jai Arjun Singh. *Jabberwork*. 9 August 2008.

_____, interviewed by Shana M. Varghese: 'I wasn't a writer, I was an academic.' *The Pioneer* 17 Jan. 2011.

_____. "Rendezvous with Manju Kapur," *Contemporary Fiction: An Anthology of Female Writers*, ed. Vandana Pathak et al.

_____, Interview by Shukmani Khorana. "Kill your Darlings at Adelaide Writers' Week," Published *Online by Estelle Tang*.

_____, 'Random Reads: An Interview.' 29 March 2011. www.randomhouseindia.com

Kavita, A. "*A Married Woman*: A Woman's Quest for a New Identity," *Rise of New Woman: Novels of Manju Kapur*, ed. Ram Sharma. 178-87.

Kauffman, Linda S. *Discourse of Desire: Gender, Genre and Epistolary Fictions*. Cornell University Press, USA, 1986.

Khair, Tabish. "Can the Subaltern Shout (and Smash?)," *World Literature Written in English*, 38: 2. 7-16. 2000.

King, Katie and King, Debra. "Body Politics and the Fictional Double," Bloomington: Indiana University Press, 2000.

Kirkpatrick, Johanna. "Women in Indian English Literature: The Question of Individuation," *Journal of South Asian Literature*, 12.

Krishnaiah, B. *Image of Woman in the Recent Indian English Fiction by Woman*. Spring, 1977.

Kirpal, Viney. *The Girl Child in 20th Century Indian Literature*. New Delhi: Sterling, 1992.

_____. *The Postmodern Indian English Novel*. Bombay: Allied, 1996.

Kishwar, Madhu and Ruth Vanita. *In Search of Answers, Indian Women's Voices from Manush*. New Delhi: Manohar, 1996.

New Delhi: Prestige International, 2011.

_____, ed. . *Flowering of Indian English Literature New Dimensions*. New Delhi: Prestige International, 2014.

Krishnamurthy, Sarala. "A New Awakening: A Tale of Lesbian Love Told with Disarming Frankness," Rev. of *A Married Woman*. *Deccan Chronicle* 5 Jan. 2003.

Krishnaswamy, Shantha. *The Women in Indian Fiction in English*. New Delhi: Asia, 1984.

Kumar, Ashok. "Manju Kapur's *The Immigrant*: Dilemma of the Second Sex," *The Novels of Manju Kapur: A Feministic Study*, ed. Ashok Kumar. New Delhi: Sarup, 2010. 63-69.

_____. "Adultery, Divorce and Custody of Children in *Custody*," *Rise of New Woman: Novels of Manju Kapur*, ed. Ram Sharma. 188-92.

_____. "Portrayal of New Women: A Study of Manju Kapur's *A Married Woman*," *Empowerment in Indian Writers in English*, ed. A.N. Prasad.

_____. "The Insurgent Female Psyche in Manju Kapur's *A Married Woman*: A Socio-Ethical Study" *Indian writings in English*, ed. Binod Mishra, Sanjay Kumar. New Delhi: Atlantic, 2006.

_____ and Roopali. "*A Married Woman*: A Saga of Postmodernistic Ethics," *The Novels of Manju Kapur*. 46-52.

Kumar, Gajendra. "Manju Kapur's *Difficult Daughters*: A Saga of Conflict and Crisis," *Indian English Literature: A New Perspective*. New Delhi: Sarup, 2001.

Kumar Harit, Satish. "Tragic Flight of the Female Protagonists in Manju Kapur's Novels," *Novels of Manju Kapur*, ed. Ashok Kumar. 93-109.

Kumar, Narendra. New *Perspectives on Indian Writing*. New Delhi: Prestige, 1997.

Kumar, Satendra. "Manju Kapur's *A Married Woman*: A Study of Woman's Struggle. *Novels of Manju Kapur*, ed. Ram Sharma. 79-88.

_____. "Manju Kapur's *Difficult Daughters*: Mission for Mental Thirst and Physical Lust," *Indian Journal of Postcolonial Literatures*. 10.2 Dec. 2010. 162-69.

Kumar, Sudhir: "I Secede, Therefore I Am: The Importance of Being Arundhati Roy," *New Quest*, 132, 1998: 356-60.

Kundu, Rama. *Indian Writing in English*. New Delhi: Atlantic, 2003.

Kurjekar, Usha. "Mother-Daughter Relationships in *Fasting, Feasting* and *Difficult Daughters*," *Contemporary Fiction: An Anthology of Female Writers*, ed. Urmila Dabir et al.

Kuruvilla, Elizabeth. "Now, Difficult Wives," Rev. of *A Married Woman*. *Hindustan Times*, 10 Dec. 2002.

Lahiri, Pradip. "Post-independence Indian Writing in English: Concern, Quest, Achievement," *The Indian Journal of English Studies*, 38. 2000.

Lal, Malashri. *The Law of the Threshold: Women Writers in Indian English*," Indian Institute of Advanced Study, Shimla, 1995.

Lerner, Gerda. *The Creation of Patriarchy*. New York and Oxford: Oxford UP. 1986.

Lomba, Ania. *Colonialism/Postcolonialism*. London and New York: Routledge, 2001.

Mahajan, Priyanka. "Evolution of New Woman: A New Facade of Indian Culture in the Select Novels of Manju Kapur and Shoba De," *International Journal of Social Science and Humanity*. 5-2. Feb. 2015.

Manohar, Murali. Indian *English Women's Fiction: A Study of Marriage, Career and Divorce*. New Delhi: Atlantic, 2007.

Mathkari. Muktaja, Jai Nimbkar's *Come Rain* as a Postcolonial novel", *Asian Quarterly*, 7, 2010.

Mehrotra, Arvind Krishana. *An Illustrated History of Indian Literature in English*. Delhi: Permanent Black, 2003.

Menon, Latika. *Female Exploitation and Women's Emancipation*. New Delhi: Kanishka. 2004.

Mehta, Sangeeta. "Women's Odyssey of Liberation in Manju Kapur's *Difficult Daughters*", *The Novels of Manju Kapur*, ed. Ashok Kumar. 126-33.

Mies, Maria. *Indian Woman and Patriarchy: Conflicts and Dilemmas of Students and Working Women*. New Delhi: Concept, 1980. 32.

Malhotra, Ruby. "Existential Images of Women in Manju Kapur's *Difficult Daughters*," *New Lights on Indian Women Novelists in English*, ed. Amar Nath Prasad. 347.

Mishra, Binod, "Obsession to Ovation: A Thematic Study of Manju Kapur's *A Married Woman*", *Studies in Woman Writers in English*, ed. Mohit Ray and Rama Kundu, Atlantic, New Delhi, 2005.

Mishra, R.K. "Psychological Exploration of Inner Mind of Indian Women: A Feminist Perspective," *New Lights on Indian Women Novelists in English*, ed. A.N. Prasad.1-19.

Mishra, Shubha. "Echoes of Realism in Manju Kapur's *Difficult Daughters*," *Contemporary Fiction*, ed. Vandana Pathak et al. 250-63.

Mitra, Reena. "Family and Society as Operative Determinants in Manju Kapur's *Difficult Daughters*," *Critical Response to Literatures in English*. New Delhi: Atlantic, 2005.

Mittapalli, Rajeshwar and P.P. Piciucco. Preface. *Studies in Indian Writing in English*. 2. New Delhi: Atlantic, 2001.

Mitter, Swasti. "Women Working Worldwide," Interview by the *International Labour Organization*. 1977.

Mohan Indra T.M.J. "Feminism Today: A Perspective" *Studies in Women Writers in English*. New Delhi: Atlantic, 2005, vol. 2.

Mohanty, Sachidananda. "Feminism Must Reach out to the World," *The Hindu*. 6 Feb. 2000.

Moi, Toril. Sexual/ Textual politics: Feminist Literary Theory. Psychology Press. 2002.

Mongia, Padmini. "Finding oneself, more or less," Rev. of *A Married Woman. The Hindu* 4 May 2003.

Mukherjee, Meenakshi. *Realism and Reality: The Novel and Society in India*. Delhi: Oxford University Press.1985.

Myles, Anita. *Feminism and the Post-Modern Indian Women Novelists in English*. New Delhi: Sarup . 2006. 348

Mythili, J.V.N.L. "Conflict and Modernity—Delineation of Man in Manju Kapur's *Difficult Daughters*," *Indian Women Writing in English: New Perspectives*, ed. S. Prasanna Sree. 156-62.

Nagarajan. M.S. "Feminist Criticism," *English Literary Criticism and Theory: An Introductory History*. Chennai: Orient Blackswan, 2012.

Naik, M.K. and Shyamala Narayan. *Indian English Fiction: A Critical Study*. New Delhi: Pencraft International, 2009.

Nayak, Bhagabat. 'Feminist Approach to Manju Kapur's *Difficult Daughters.' Feminism in Indian Writing in English*, ed. Amar Nath Prasad and S.K. Paul.

_____. "Love and Longing in Manju Kapur's *Difficult Daughters*," *Indian English Literature*. Vol. 3, ed. Basavaraj Naikar. Atlantic, New Delhi. 2002. 156-65.

Neelakantan, Shailaja. "A Tale of Two Women," Rev. of *A Married Woman. Asia Times* 19 April 2003.

Nimbkar. Jai, *Temporary answers*, Disha Books, 1947,

_____. *A Joint Venture*. New Delhi: Penguin, 1988.

_____ *Come Rain*, Orient Longman. Disha Books, 1993.

Nirmala, K. "*Difficult Daughters*: A Critique of Filial Relations," *Indian Journal of Postcolonial Literatures*. 1.2. Jan-Jun, 2001: 58-65.

Nitonde, Rohidas. *In Search of a Feminist Writer*. Bloomington: Partridge, 2014.

Nubile, Clara. "The Danger of Gender Caste Class and Gender", *Contemporary Indian Women's Writing*. New Delhi: Sarup, 2003.

Palmer, Paulina. *Contemporary Women's Fiction: Narrative Practice and Feminist Theory*. London: Harvester Wheat Shelf, 1989.

Parameswaran, Uma. Rev. of *Difficult Daughters*. *World Literature Today*. 1999: 392-93.

Párraga, Javier Martín. "Manju Kapur's 'difficult' narrative: the case of *Difficult Daughters*," *Permanent India Studies Seminar*, University of Córdoba, Spain, 7-9 Mar. 2007.

_____. "Manju Kapur's *Difficult Daughters* and the Deconstruction of Traditional Binary Oppositions," *India in the World*, ed. Cristina M. Gámez Fernández and Antonia Navarro-Tejero. 183-89.

Patel, M.F. *Feminism in Contemporary Indian Women Writers*. New Delhi: Daya Publishing. 2011.

Pathak, R.S. *Modern Indian Novel in English*. New Delhi: Creative, 1999.

Pathak, Vandana. "Rendezvous with Manju Kapur," *Contemporary Fictions*, ed. Vandana Pathak, et al. New Delhi: Sarup, 2008.

_____, Urmila Dabir and Shubha Mishra, ed. *Contemporary Fiction: An Anthology of Female Writers*. New Delhi: Sarup, 2008.

Pawar. M.S. *New Women Novelists with New Horizon*. Shruti, Jaipur, 2011.

Piciucco, P.P,. *A Companion to Indian English Fiction*. New Delhi: Atlantic. 2004.

Pisharoty, Sangeeta Barooah. "About Home and Hearth," Rev. of *Home. The Hindu* 1 April 2006.

Poojatolani. "Written from the Heart: *Difficult Daughters*" *Manju Kapoor Review*, 10 Aug. 2004.

Prasad, A.N. and Malik Rajiv K. *Indian English Poetry and Fiction: Critical Elucidations*. New Delhi: Sarup, 2007.

Prasad, R. Dagwale and Mrinalini S. Gopal. "Inequality in Marriage: *A Study of Temporary Answers*", *International Indexed and Referred Journal*, 5.42. 16, 2012.

P. Sudha Shree. "*Difficult Daughters*: Travails in Self-Identity," *Indian Women Writing in English: New Perspectives*, ed. S. Prasanna Sree.

Pushpa Lata. "From Clarity to Chaos: A Complex Pattern of Journey in Manju Kapur's *Difficult Daughters*," *Indian Writings in English*, ed. Binod Mishra, Sanjay Kumar. New Delhi: Atlantic, 2006.

Rajan, Rajeswari Sunder. "The Feminist Plot and the Nationalist Allegory: Home and World in Two Indian Women's Novels in English," *Modern Fiction Studies*, 39.1, 1993. 71-92.

Rajpal, Sujata. Rev of *Home* by Manju Kapur. *Coffee Break*, 3 Sept. 2011.

Rajput, Kalpana. "The Self-Syndrome in the Novels of Manju Kapur," *Novels of Manju Kapur*, ed. Ashok Kumar. 110-25.

Rastogi, Pallavi. "Manju Kapur," *South Asian Novelists in English: An A-to-Z guide*, ed. Jaina C. Sanga. Westport: Greenwood Press, 2003.

Rao, Mallikarjuna and Rajeshwar Mittapalli. *Indian English Fiction*. New Delhi: Atlantic, 2009.

"Readability of Manju Kapur's *Difficult Daughters*," *The Commonwealth Review*. 12.1. 2000-2001: 62-70.

Reale, Michelle. "Meandering Tale Misses the Mark," Rev. of *A Married Woman*. *Indiacurrents*.

Rishi, Jaydeep. "Mother-Daughter Relationship in Manju Kapur's *Difficult Daughters*," *Indian English Novel in the Nineties*, ed. Sheo Bhushan Shukla and Aru Shukla, New Delhi Sarup . 2002.

Rollason, Christopher. "Not Exactly like Home," Rev. of *Home*, *Seva Bharati Journal of English Studies* 5. Feb 2009.

_____. "To build or to destroy: History and the individual in Manju Kapur's *A Married Woman*," *20th European Conference on Modern South Asian Studies*, University of Manchester, 8-11 Jul. 2008.

_____. "Women on the Margins: Reflections on Manju Kapur's *Difficult Daughters*," *Novels of Manju Kapur*, ed. Ashok Kumar, 1-9.

Roy, Manju. "Readability of *Difficult Daughters*," *Commonwealth Review*, 12: 1, 2001. 62-69.

_____. "Language and Style in Manju Kapur's *Difficult Daughters*," *Indian Journal of Postcolonial Literature* . Jun. 2010: 147-53.

Roy, Nilanjana S. "She said, He said," Rev. of *A Married Woman. Outlook*, 23 Dec. 2002.

Sah, Binda. "Quest for Identity in *The Shadow Lines*," *Contemporary Indian writing in English: Trends, Concept and Techniques*, ed. Nigamananda Das. New Delhi: Adhayan, 2007. 147-51.

Saharan, Asha. "Body as an Ideological Site: Representation of Female Bodies in Manju Kapur's Fiction," 76, 39 Dec 2013.

Saharan, Asha. "Perspective of Body in Manju Kapur's Fiction," *Muse India*, 62, July 2013.

Salvador, Dora Sales. "The Memory of Desire in Manju Kapur's *Difficult Daughters*: In Past and Future Tense," *Memory, Imagination and Desire in Contemporary Anglo-American Literature and Film*, ed. Constanza del Río and Luis M. García Mainar. Heidelberg: Universitätsverlag, 2004. 121-30.

_____ and Christopher Rollason. "Critical Commentary on Manju Kapur, Extracts from a Work-in-Progress" *The Atlantic Literary Review*, Oct.-Dec. 2003. 219-48.

Sandhu, Sarabjit. *Image of Woman in the Novels of Shashi Deshpande*. New Delhi: Prestige, 1991. 20.

Sarangi, Jaydeep, et al. *Indian Women Writing in English*. Delhi: Gnosis, 2008.

Sethi, Anita. "Home is where the ghosts are," Rev. of *Home*. *The Sunday Times* (London) 16 Apr. 2006.

Sethi, Honey, Seema Dhillon. "The Womanly Observation by Manju Kapur," *International Journal of Innovations in Engineering and Technology*. 1, 3. Oct 2012. 53-58.

Sharma, Gajendra Dutt and Rakhi Maheshwari. "Woman in quest for Sexual Freedom and Emancipation in Manju Kapur's *A Married Woman*," *Novels of Manju Kapur*, ed. Ram Sharma. 141-46.

Sharma, K. Usha. "Psychological Supplication of women—Imposed or Self-Induced? A Study of Manju Kapur's *Difficult Daughters*", *Psycho Dynamics of Women in the Postmodern Literature*, ed. S. Prasanna Sree. New Delhi: Sarup, 2008.

Sharma, Ram. "Immigrant Experiences in Manju Kapur's Novel *The Immigrant*," *Novels of Manju Kapur: A Feministic Study*, ed. Ashok Kumar. New Delhi: Sarup, 2010, 22-30.

Sharma, Sudarshan. "Manju Kapur's Nowhere Women," *New Perspectives on Indian English Writings*, ed. Malati Agrawal. New Delhi: Atlantic, 2007.

Showalter, Elaine, ed. "*The New Feminist Criticism: Essay on Women Literature and Theory*," New York: Pantheon, 1985.

_____. "Feminist Criticism in the Wilderness," *Modern Literary Theory: A Reader*, ed. David Lodge, London: Longman, 1985. 333.

Shree, Sudha. "*Difficult Daughters*: Travails in Self-Identity," *Indian Women Writing in English*, ed. Prasanna Sree. 163-68.

Shrinivas, M.N. *Social Change in Modern India*. New Delhi: Orient Longman, 1972.

Singh, Alka. "A Tempting Trap: Manju Kapur's *A Married Woman*," *Contemporary Indian Writing in English*, ed. Malati Agrawal.

_____. "Exploring Possibilities Beyond Traditions: Manju Kapur's *Difficult Daughters*," *Discussing Indian Women Writers: Some Feminist Issues*, ed. Alessandro Monti and R.K. Dhawan. New Delhi: Prestige. 2002. 132-38.

Singh, Anita. "Stairway to the Stars: Women Writing in Contemporary Indian English Fiction," *The Women Question in the Contemporary Indian Women Writing in English*, ed. Indu Swami. New Delhi: Sarup, 2000.

Singh, Avadhesh K. *Contemporary Indian Fiction in English*. New Delhi: Creative, 1993.

Singh, Jai Arjun. "An Interview with Manju Kapur," *Remapping the Female Map: Jhumpa Lahiri and Manju Kapur*. Jaipur: Yking. 2012. 178-82.

Singh, Mayank and Austen Soofi. Rev. of *Home*. DESICRITICS website, 24 Apr. 2006.

___. Rev. of *The Immigrant. Hindustan Times*, 1 Nov. 2008.

Singh, Shaleen Kumar. "Tradition versus Modernity in *Difficult Daughters*," *Novels of Manju Kapur*, ed. Ashok Kumar. 10-14.

Singh, Shubha. "Understated prose brings out the angst of the immigrant," Rev. of *The Immigrant. South Asia Mail*, 2008.

Singh, Smriti. "The New Woman in Post-Independence Novels: An Emerging Image" *Studies in Women Writers in English*. New Delhi: Atlantic, 2005.

Singh, Veena. "How Difficult are Difficult Daughters: *Sunlight on a Broken Column* and *Difficult Daughters* as Female Bildungsroman," *Contemporary Indian Literature and Expositions*, ed. Santosh Gupta. Jaipur: Rawat, 2000.

Sinha, B.P. "Identity Crisis: A Feminist Perspective," *Women Empowerment in Indian Writers in English*, ed. Amarnath Prasad.

Sinha, Shalini. "The Conflict Between the Roots and Wings in Manju Kapur's *A Married Woman*: A Critical Perspective," *Feminism in Indian Writing in English*, ed. A.N. Prasad and S.K. Paul. 201-7.

Sinha, Sunita. "Discovery of Daring and Desire in Manju Kapur's Fiction," *Postcolonial Women Writers: New Perspectives*. New Delhi: Atlantic, 2008.

Spivak, Gayatri Chakravarty. *Can the Subaltern Speak? Colonial Discourse and Postcolonial Theory*. Harvest Wheatsheaf, 1994.

_____. Interview by Bulan Lahiri. "Speaking to Spivak," 6 Feb. 2011. *The Hindu*. 6-9.

Sree, S. Prasanna. "Virmati: A Tributary of Suffering as Reflected through Ida's Eyes in Manju Kapur's *Difficult Daughters*," *New Lights on Indian Women Novelists in English*, ed. A.N. Prasad.

Sridevi, R. "Emergence of Manju Kapur as Feminist in *Difficult Daughters* and *A Married Woman*," *Language in India*, 12:10, Oct. 2012. 424-29.

Srivastava, Sarika. "The Voice of Protest in the Novels of Manju Kapur," *Novels of Manju Kapur*, ed. Ashok Kumar, 70-84.

Srivastava, Shilpi Rishi. "A Quest for Identity in Manju Kapur's *Difficult Daughters*," *Novels of Manju Kapur*, ed. Ashok Kumar, 15-21

_____. "Feminist Consciousness in Manju Kapur's Novels," *New Lights on Indian Women Novelists in English*, ed. Amarnath Prasad.

Srivastava, Swati and Fatima Rizvi. "The Concept of Self in the Creations of Manju Kapur," *IUP Journal of English Studies*, 5. March & June 2010. 42-49.

Sterling, Anne. *Sexing the Body: Gender Politics and the Construction of Sexuality*. U.SA.: Basic Books, 2000.

Susan, Nisha. "The Mistress of Mildness," Rev. of *Custody*. *Tehelka*, 8.12. 26 Mar. 2011.

Tripathy, P: "Claiming Voice: Women in Manju Kapur's *Home*," *Reflections*, 7, Jan. and July 2008. 162-68.

Uniyal, Ranu. "'Craving for Intensity beyond Intelligent Survival': Women in the Novels of Ruchira Mukerjee and Manju Kapur," *Novels of Manju Kapur*, ed. Ashok Kumar. 85-92.

Vasudev, S, "Homosexuality," *India Today*, July-Aug. 2004. 48-52.

Verma, Anuradha. "Manju Kapur's Astha: *A Married Woman*," *New Perspectives on Indian English Writings*, ed. Malti Agarwal. 51-56.

Verma, M.R. and A.K. Sharma. *Reflections on Indian English Fiction*. New Delhi: Atlantic, 2004.

Verma, Manju. "Manju Kapur's *Difficult Daughters*: A Study of her Women Characters," *Women on Women*, ed. Amina Amin, K.L. Rajyashree, Gita Chaudhary. Jaipur: Rawat, 2006.

Warake, N.S. "Quest for Identity and Survival: A Study of Manju Kapur's *Home*," *Journal of Literature, Culture and Media Studies*. 2.4. 2010. 268-77.

West, Candace and Don H. Zimmerman. "Doing Gender," *Gender: A Sociological Reader*, ed. Stevi Jackson and Sue Sott. London: Routledge, 2002.

Wollstonecraft, Mary. *A Vindication of the Rights of Woman, with Strictures on Political and Moral Subjects*. N.Y.: A.J. Matsell, 1833.

Woolf, Virgina. "Professions for Women," *Women and Writing*, ed. Michele Barret London. Harcourt, 1979.

_____. *A Room of One's Own*. USA: Editions Artisan Devereaux, 1929.

Younger, Beth. "Learning Curves: Body Image and Female Sexuality" *in Young Adult Literature*. USA: Scarecrow Press, 2009.